"Zuck My Life"

A Guide for advertising on the internet's most frustrating platform

Rob and Lynne Alfano

Foreword

"You can't scale-free"

This is advice I have given to entrepreneurs for years. Yes, organic traffic and referrals are awesome, but you are not in control of how quickly you can generate leads or sales. I am excited for more people to learn about paid advertising through Rob & Lynne's unique way of delivering. From spending and making millions of dollars through advertising I can tell you that Rob & Lynne know what they are doing and you are in good hands.

I teach network marketers faith-based mindset and leadership principles that work and MANY of the students and clients I have connected with came from paid ads. I have personally used Rob & Lynne for ads and they have been not only a tremendous help and demonstrated their expertise, but their care for clients is bar none! Enjoy this book and get your business scaling through ads!

Ray Higdon
Best Selling Author and Keynote Speaker

Congratulations on taking the bold step to take action and finally figure out Facebook & Instagram advertising. In this book, we will do our best to help teach you everything you need to know to get started, without losing your mind or your sense of humor. I get it because I have been there. The world of pixels, algorithms, objectives, creative and ad sets can seem like a labyrinth designed by an evil scientist whose sole purpose is to torture you until the end of time. But fear not! I wrote this book to be your light-hearted, simplified, and impactful guide through the maze while sprinkling in some humor along the way. Because let's face it, we could all use a laugh or two when we're knee-deep in analytics wondering why your ad for closet organization is being shown to teenage surfers living out of a van. Taking the initiative to invest in learning how to run your ads is not only courageous but can also lead to huge improvements in your business. I believe that Facebook & Instagram advertising, even with their overly confusing user interfaces, privacy lawsuits, and government intervention, is still the single best platform to advertise for any small business. So buckle up, get ready to live, learn, and laugh your way to Facebook ad success.

Introduction - Why We All Need a Little Humor in Advertising

How to Use This Book: A Light-hearted Approach

This isn't your typical self-help guidebook on Facebook advertising. I didn't want this to be another one of those DIY manuals that the average business owner buys thinking it will help, but ends up reading like IKEA instructions written in Klingon. Think of this book more as a TED Talk given by a comedian who's spent way too much time in Facebook Ads Manager. Kind of like if your life coach and your sarcastic best friend had a baby and that baby decided to write a book about Facebook Ads. Each chapter is filled with tips, tricks, and strategies that can make a difference for your business, all while keeping things light and entertaining. It would be close to impossible to write a step-by-step manual on how to do everything possible with Facebook ads anyway because there is no single "right" way to advertise for everyone. The goal is to equip you with the knowledge necessary to figure it out for yourself, then test and learn your way to success. You can read in order if you are a beginner, skip around if you have messed around with ads before and you are looking to expand your knowledge, or use the book as a coaster in your office. Although I hope you'll do the first two more than the last.

At the end of each chapter, you will find questions designed to help you think more in-depth about the important information along with key takeaways. We would love for you to join our free Facebook group facebook.com/groups/fbinsta101 and post your responses. We're eager to connect with you and explore how we can enhance your understanding as well as assist you in your journey.

Disclaimer: Mark Zuckerberg Isn't Personally Ruining Your Ads (But It's Fun to Pretend).

Before we dive in, let's set the record straight. Despite the tongue-in-cheek tone of this book, Mark Zuckerberg is not personally out to get your small business. It's the exact opposite. Small business advertising represents 75% of Facebook's 70

Billion dollars in annual ad revenue. Just imagine what that number would be if the service was easier to use for the everyday business person. If Mark and the Facebook Engineers knew exactly what to do to make it easier for everyone, they would change it immediately. But, therein lies the problem. It is impossible to make something work for everyone when you have hundreds of millions of people using it daily.

However, blaming 'Zuck' when you can't figure out what to do or when your ads don't perform can be a humorous coping mechanism. It's like yelling at the TV when your favorite team is losing…therapeutic but ineffective. This book, on the other hand, will aim to be both therapeutic and effective, helping you navigate the pitfalls and landmines of Facebook advertising without losing your mind or your sense of humor.
This book is NOT endorsed by Meta in any way, and all opinions expressed in the book are solely of the authors and do not express the views or opinions of Meta, Facebook, Instagram, WhatsApp, Oculus, or Meta-owned subsidiaries.

So let's begin this journey. May your ads be ever in your favor and may the 'Zucks' be few.

Chapter 1:
Why We Decided to Write This Zucking Book

My name is Rob Alfano. I am a former Facebooker (or Metamate after the rebrand) and have spent over 20 years in the digital marketing industry. I've worked at companies of all sizes from startups to Fortune 50's in many different industries. I've seen it all. Navigating the corporate world has always seemed like an odd and uncomfortable fit for me. Even though I managed to be successful, and work my way up to one of the most sought-after jobs at one of the biggest companies on the planet, I never really felt like I fit in anywhere. What you may not know is that I did not take the traditional path of getting good grades in high school, going to a prestigious university, and scoring an awesome internship from my roommate's dad's fraternity brother. The truth is I barely graduated from high school, spent 3 years in the military straightening out my life, jumping out of a plane or two along the way, and worked full-time in retail while I earned my community college degree. You don't meet many people in Silicon Valley that follow that route.

When I first began my career in digital marketing I was embarrassed and ashamed to talk about my non-traditional background. Luckily, after making my way through a few positions and companies, I started to see that struggling my way into the industry was a superpower. Most of my employees, colleagues, and even my bosses, never had experiences that allowed them to see the world through the lens of the average everyday person. Throughout my life, I never had enough time, money, or resources to do things the way they should be done, so I had to learn to get scrappy and make it work. It takes some young employees years to figure this out and some never get it. Being the scrappy go-getter was my brand.

But after years of hustling, hopping from company to company, and doing my best to help companies succeed, I realized that it is not always about what you do at a company that matters. You have to play the game with bosses, employees, departments, and corporate structures to get ahead. I had zero interest in this kind of existence, not that there's anything wrong with those who do, it just was not for me. I knew that the uncomfortable feeling I had was a nudge to do something different, something outside the corporate world, but nothing ever hit me with enough force to cause me to take action. Then I started telling people where I worked, and the nudge became a full-on shove.

I honestly never knew just how many people had issues with Facebook products until I started working for Meta. When I was first hired I didn't hesitate to tell anyone where I worked, who doesn't like to brag a little from time to time, but I soon realized that feeding my ego came with a side of "Please help me" from literally everyone who heard me utter the words "I work for Facebook". What surprised me is how many people wanted and needed help with Ads for their small businesses, side hustles, or entrepreneurial ventures. I heard from people in all stages of confusion. Some people I met wanted to advertise on Facebook but had no idea where to start, others were intimidated by the complexity of the tools, and a few had even tried it themselves but ended up spending a bunch of money with no results. After I explained that I worked for the business education group, people nearly lost their minds and wanted to hire me right there while we were talking in someone's driveway drinking a beer. But, I wasn't yet in that mindset. I would always let people know that there was free content and tools available to anyone on Meta-owned education websites. But to my surprise, most if not all people I talked to had no idea those resources even existed. This was hard to believe because I saw the reports showing that hundreds of millions of people visited the Meta help and education websites each year. How could I personally meet so many people who did not know how or where to get help when there are thousands of pages of information on the web? There were hundreds of courses, four Meta-owned educational websites, and thousands of videos, so how are there so many users still struggling? After thinking about it for a while the answer became pretty obvious. Even with all of these resources, videos, gurus, books, and classes on the web, the demand for people who wanted to advertise on Facebook was far greater than the supply of help on how to do it well.

That is when the realization became crystal clear. Facebook had done a great job solving the problem of accessibility and awareness of a great advertising platform, but the real problem was that most "average everyday users" had no idea what to do, why to do it, or how to be successful. It's like getting the opportunity to play the most prestigious golf course in the world weeks after you first learn how to play. You won't appreciate it, it won't be much fun, and you will most likely be really bad at it. Sure, it is easy to blame your golf clubs, the course, or the weather, but in the end the real issue is that you just weren't prepared for that level of play.

My wife Lynne is my partner, not just in life, but in business as well. When I started to notice the overwhelming need for help, I told her that we needed to start a business focused on helping small businesses with Facebook & Instagram ads. She very kindly reminded me that she had been saying that we should start a business together for years and that I was the one who needed to be convinced. She was right, I didn't have to convince her to open our own business because she has been an entrepreneur her whole life and regularly urged me to stop complaining about my corporate job and go out on my own. So, our new business venture was born, and like the first time I held the child in my arms, I had no clue what I was supposed to do.

We didn't know it at the time, but we had a very complementary set of skills. Lynne brings a unique dual perspective: as an avid Facebook user, she understands the consumer mindset, and as a seasoned business owner utilizing social media for lead generation and sales, she possesses invaluable business insights. My dirty little secret is that as much as I know about marketing, digital strategy, and Facebook ads, I don't know much about using Facebook socially. I guess it's not a secret anymore now that I wrote it in a book. I am a work in progress in that regard, but when it comes to posting, sharing, liking, tagging, groups, and more, Lynne is the expert. She is also an absolute wizard inside the Ads user interface. Not to mention the fact that she spent over 8 years as a high school teacher and 20 years as a coach, so she is no stranger to education. You will hear from Lynne throughout the book as she will jump in here and there and offer her "Lynne-sights" to make sure I am keeping my ego and silliness in check.

Hey everyone, Lynne here. Wanted to jump in and give you some Lynne-sight on how I learned Facebook and Instagram ads. It's important because I was on a journey much like you. I knew I needed to learn, and had the time and motivation, but had no idea where to start. When Rob approached me with the idea, I began by taking the courses provided by Meta. After a few days of bland text-based lessons, I just couldn't get through it. That's right, we're talking about the very website that Rob was working on every day to help people like me learn ads. So I'm sure you could imagine the conversations we had at the dinner table of "Why is it like this" or "Why isn't this easier". He loved the "user" feedback. I then moved on and tried using another education platform that was partnered with Meta. It was a little better, but still didn't feel like it was putting me on a path where I could apply this in real-life scenarios. Finally, I had to go elsewhere and take a bunch of third-party independent courses on the subject. My personal experience solidified for us that there is a significant need for guidance and education. With our collective skills and strengths, we knew we could help people learn how to effectively navigate the system better than the resources out there today.

When we took the leap and decided to lean into a business focused on helping small businesses with ads, Lynne and I thought the best way to do it was to open a Facebook ad agency. The demand was certainly there as we were immediately flooded with small business clients through referrals from people we knew. They all had heard of the power of social media for business, especially Facebook. They knew if they could just get ads going, their business could change overnight. This was and is still true in theory, but in reality, Facebook campaigns take time to get right, and a lot of these small businesses could not afford to pay for the time it took to work out the kinks without getting immediate profitable returns (which is very rare these days). This was one of the other big factors in writing the book. I knew these businesses needed help, but they just couldn't afford to hire an agency or employees to do what needed to be done to be truly successful.

We went back to the drawing board because we knew there were so many businesses that needed help, we just had to figure out how to do it better, faster, and cheaper. After racking our brains for weeks we concluded that the answer was education and training. If we could just teach businesses how to run ads that were successful on a small scale, they could grow into a bigger more profitable business that could then afford the help from a third party. Like any business moving into a new field, the first step was for us to survey the market and check out the Facebook & Instagram Ads help and education available for small businesses.

There is no shortage of training out there. There are books, online courses, videos, workbooks, websites, blogs, and even in-person training. While all of the training offered great information, we noticed a common theme. Most, if not all of them, were mind-numbingly boring! I immediately knew how we would differentiate ourselves in the market. I knew that if we were going to educate entrepreneurs and scrappy go-getters on how to do something difficult, I had to make it as lively and fun as it was informative. How the heck was I supposed to do that? Zuck my life!

Questions: Post Your Answers in our Free group at facebook.com/groups/fbinsta101
What made you want to get the book and learn more about Facebook and Instagram advertising?

Have you tried to advertise at all before? If yes, how do you think you did?

What would Facebook Ad success look like to you?

Chapter 2:
Why Facebook? Seriously, Why?

In the era of countless social media platforms and advertising channels, you may be asking yourself, "Why Facebook?" Well, buckle up, because this chapter will show you how Facebook is more than just a platform for sharing memes, proudly posting your children's fifth-place soccer trophies, and stalking your ex. You'll learn what I think are the biggest advantages of using Facebook advertising: Reach, Targeting, Discovery, and Community.

Reach
With over 2.8 billion monthly active users, Facebook is the single largest social media site on this planet. If you add in Instagram, that number jumps to almost 5 billion. Ever met someone without a Facebook account? They are rare but easy to find…just look for the tin foil hats. As a business owner, it honestly doesn't matter how you feel about Facebook or the people who use it, because to you what matters is that there are almost 3 billion people intently staring at a screen scrolling for something interesting. On average, people scroll for 108 minutes a day. If your phone spits out a receipt as long as you scrolled on social media in a day, that receipt would be just a little longer than 4 football fields! I'm sure you hear people say they don't pay attention to ads on Facebook & Instagram, and when you do, tell them I have a unicorn in my backyard I'd like to sell them. Even a seasoned marketer like myself has fallen victim to social media ads as evidenced by the small light-up replica home owned by Clark Griswold from Christmas Vacation that graces the mantle of my home during the holidays. Like Liam Neeson said, "Facebook Ads will look for you, Facebook Ads will find you, and Facebook Ads will make you buy something."

Targeting
Ah, Facebook Ads targeting, the modern equivalent of reading someone's diary, but with their full permission of course *wink*. If conventional advertising is the person on the corner yelling from a

megaphone, Facebook Ads is that friend who knows exactly what to get you for your birthday and your secret love for RuPaul's Drag Race and Nickelback. It walks the line between useful and creepy, much like a plain white van.

Facebook's ad targeting capabilities are controversial but effective. Imagine you sell handmade alien-shaped soap. How would you know there is an audience for that? Better yet, how would you find that audience? Facebook, that's where. There are so many interests listed in the ads interface. There is no exhaustive list of all interests you can target, the only way you can find out if the targeting is available is by doing random searching. I feel like if they did have a list it would take hours to scroll and read them. I would also be shocked if you didn't find the interest that is exactly what you are looking for, or close. So finding the 52 people in North America who are into hygiene and extraterrestrial affairs is as easy as doing a simple type-in search.

Facebook knows when you're sleeping, it knows when you're awake. It knows if you've been bad or good... okay, it's not Santa, but close enough. I did get you to start singing the song in your head though. All Christmas aside, another amazing targeting feature on Facebook is that you can target ads to people based on their life events. Got engaged? Here's an ad for wedding planners. Just break up? How about some ice cream delivery services? Some of these life events can be crucial pieces of information to find your target audience. One of the best examples of this is the "recently moved" segment. Most users will update their city on Facebook when they move, which is a critical signal to businesses that are most relevant when you are new to an area like cable companies, organizers, houseware vendors, food delivery, the list goes on and on. Do you think your business could benefit from targeting someone who has a new job, graduated college, just had a baby, is planning to travel, or just retired?

If you want more customers, wouldn't it be awesome to clone them? Facebook might not be Hogwarts, but it does have some magic tricks up its sleeve. One of these nifty spells is called the "Lookalike Audience." And no, it doesn't mean Facebook will make copies of your customers, but it is pretty cool how they do it. Facebook realized that if people who buy your products like the outdoors own a cat, watch Monday Night Football, and live in the Midwest…Chances are, other people who have similar interests and profiles will buy your products too. All you have to do is provide a list of your customers and some data to identify them and Presto, you have a targeted list of people who are a lot like your current customers.

Ever visited a website, put something in a shopping cart, or searched for something then had it follow you around on Facebook like a lost puppy? That's not stalking, it's retargeting. It's a gentle way of saying, "Hey, remember us? You still need that inflatable unicorn pool float, don't you?" While these ads could strike you as annoying or creepy, they are an amazing tool for marketers if done right. Most advertisers use them simply to remind people of a product or website, but smart marketers will use them to amplify an offer or show prospects different images with stronger calls to action. That is where you can stand out as an advertiser. You have to do things the majority of your competition is not doing. If you love targeting and want to hear more, don't worry. There will be a whole chapter on all the ways you can target your ads to the right people.

Discovery
This may get a little psychological, but it is for a good cause. Knowledge is broken into three distinct parts. Things you know, things you know you don't know, and things you don't know you don't know. One of the most amazing opportunities you have using

Facebook Ads is the ability to Introduce people to products and services they don't know they don't know. When I was a kid back in the 1980's I remember how awesome it was to watch late-night infomercials or see print ads in obscure magazines that show you things you never knew existed…and then immediately needed to own. If you were anything like me, you were captivated by the things you never knew you needed like the Chia Pet, Ginsu Knives, or Mr. Microphone. In today's world, so much of our discovery happens through searching. But, to find something by searching, you have to know it exists! Also, to find something you want to learn or solve some problem you have, you have to know that you don't know or don't have that thing. What about the stuff you don't know, you don't know you need? If you aren't in an industry or selling a product that has been around since the 1900s, the likelihood of someone not knowing your product or service exists is very high. That is why it is crucial to be running ads on platforms that I call "Discovery Engines" with Facebook & Instagram being the most popular. There is so much value associated with being the first brand people see when they learn of a new product or service because they will always associate it with you. So the next time you are scrolling aimlessly through your Facebook feed keep a lookout for the Avocado holder and beard straightener ads and remember, that could be your product or service too!

Lynnesight: Anyone else thinking of the scene from Friends when Phoebe says "They don't know that we know they know we know"? While it may not be great for our bank account, I've purchased many things that I didn't know existed but just had to have! At the very least, it's entertaining to learn about all the different products and services available, even if I don't purchase them right then and there. I know that down the road I may have the need or know someone who may benefit from a recommendation.

Community

Have you ever tried to get a billboard to call you? Or tell a TV commercial that you like their offer? Or slap a heart sticker on the side of a bus ad while it is driving down the street? I hope your answer to all three of those questions is "no", and if they are "yes", please message me privately on Facebook because I have to hear that story. Those questions were purposely ridiculous to show you some of the things Facebook Ads offer that other ad platforms do not. Facebook's sole purpose as a technology is to build community, and the ads platform is no different. Unlike other advertising choices, you can use your ads not just to showcase your product and service but to engage with people interested in working with you.

The Community features on Facebook present a treasure trove of opportunities for small business advertisers by offering a unique blend of engagement, customer loyalty, and brand advocacy that is hard to replicate anywhere else. At its core, Facebook's Community features allow businesses to create an environment where they can interact with their audience in a more intimate and targeted manner. This direct line of communication fosters a sense of belonging among customers, turning a business page from a mere promotional platform into a vibrant community hub.

One of the most significant benefits of utilizing Facebook's Community features is the ability to build and nurture relationships with customers. In this digital age, consumers crave authentic interactions with brands. Facebook provides a platform for these interactions, allowing businesses to engage in real-time conversations, respond to customer inquiries, and gather feedback. This level of engagement can transform casual customers into loyal brand advocates. When customers feel heard and valued, they are more likely to develop a strong connection with the brand, leading to increased customer retention and word-of-mouth referrals.

Moreover, Facebook Communities serve as a valuable source of customer insights. By observing and participating in community discussions, small business advertisers can gain a deeper understanding of their audience's needs, preferences, and pain points. This information is gold dust for tailoring marketing strategies, product development, and improving customer service. It enables businesses to make data-driven decisions based on direct customer feedback, rather than assumptions or market trends. This closeness to the customer base not only helps in crafting more effective advertising campaigns but also in creating products and services that truly resonate with the target audience.

Lastly, a well-managed Facebook Community can significantly enhance a brand's online presence and organic reach. Engaging content, customer testimonials, and active discussions within the community are likely to be shared beyond the immediate group, expanding the brand's visibility. This organic growth is invaluable, particularly for small businesses with limited advertising budgets. By investing time and effort into building a thriving Facebook Community, small businesses can create a self-sustaining ecosystem where members not only engage with the brand but also become active participants in promoting it.

Lynnesight: Community interaction on Facebook can refer to many different things. You can interact through a business page, a Facebook group, or even on the ads themselves. On a Facebook Business page customers, or potential customers, can write reviews, comment, and ask questions on your posts, or even better, message you directly. I take advantage of the messaging feature often. If I can get good, quick information from a business with excellent customer service, that is likely who I will purchase from or hire. It's also who will have a better chance of keeping me as a customer or client in the future. In a Facebook group, users can come together to make posts, ask questions, or comment in a more specific and comfortable environment. Other members of the group can offer suggestions and advice to help each other which makes the community even better. On an ad itself, people can comment directly to ask questions and interact with the business before ever going to their page or into their group. In a world of noise and chaos, the more opportunity you give users to connect with businesses directly, the better. Facebook offers many ways to make that happen which is why it is one of the most powerful platforms to grow your business.

Questions: Post Your Answers in our Free group at facebook.com/groups/fbinsta101
Tell us what specialized targeting, life event, or characteristic you found most interesting. Do you think you could use it to get ads in front of your ideal target market?

Do you believe that Facebook ads can help people learn about your product or service? If so, how?

Are you having great conversations with your target audience? What community features do you think you can use to improve that for your business?

<u>**Key Takeaways:**</u>

Facebook and Instagram have massive reach, so is it almost guaranteed that the audience for your business is using the platform

Facebook offers targeting options that are unlike any other small business advertising tool.

Facebook is a great platform to get people to discover your business or service as ads and content are delivered to people based on what they might like, not on what they know.

Facebook offers businesses a way to connect and build community with their audience through business pages, comments on ads, and messaging capability.

Chapter 3:
Oh, Zuck! I Forgot To set up a Facebook Business Page

If you want to advertise on Facebook, you need to first build or have built a Facebook Business Page. Your business page is essentially the Facebook profile for your business. Now while you won't have to worry about the relationship status for your business, although I am sure it IS complicated, you do have to take time to set up the page the right way. Most of our small business clients either don't have a page or just do the minimum to get the page running, which is a missed opportunity. You have to make sure that you fill out each section completely, put in as much information as possible, and use high-quality original images. When you run ads, a good amount of people will click through to your Facebook business page to "check you out". The impression they get when they see the page will have a big impact on how they feel about your business. You want to have that mindset when you are creating the page. If someone looked at your business page for 30 seconds, what impression would they have? Would they swipe right on your business? Or does it look like you did the minimum amount of work to get this done?

Disclaimer

Facebook changes its user interfaces often and uses personalization to individualize the look and feel based on how people individually use the system. What you see on your screen may likely be anywhere from slightly to completely different from what I am describing in the book. The components will be mostly the same, but the look and feel, locations, and naming conventions change often enough to keep us all on our toes. If you encounter this issue, hop into the free group and let us know, and we will get you back on the right track.

facebook.com/groups/fbinsta101

If you have not built a Facebook Business Page, then make sure you follow this chapter closely to get all the information you need to build a high-performing page. If you already have a page, look for the tips and suggestions contained in these sections so you can go back and make updates or edits.

First things first, navigate to Facebook. In typical Facebook fashion, there are multiple ways to create your business page. If you look on the left-hand side next to your news feed, you will see a few choices listed under your profile. Find and click "Pages" and then click "Create new page". Or, on the top menu bar in the upper right-hand section of the page, you will see a matrix of dots that look like a tic-tac-toe board. Click that, and under the expanded menu for "Social" you will see "Pages". Click "Pages" and "Create new Page".

There are only three things you will need to do to "officially" create your business page: name it, pick a category, and fill out a bio. Here are some tips for each section:

Page Name - This is the name of your business (obviously). Don't use the word "official", improper capitalization, unnecessary punctuation, or slogans like "The Best Cafe in New York". These things violate Facebook's terms of service and can cause your page to be taken down. If you are a local business, this is a good place to put a geographic identifier that gives your potential customers an idea of where your services are available. For example, you could use "Jim's Appliance Repair - Brooklyn, NY". If you are an agent of a larger business, like insurance, sales, or real estate, make sure you include your name so people know it is your specific page and not the main corporate page.

Category - Facebook allows you to pick up to three categories to describe your business. There are a lot of categories to choose from and you have to type to find them. Be sure to be as descriptive as possible. For example, you can pick "Restaurant", "Asian Restaurant", and "Cantonese Restaurant" so be sure to look for detailed categories first and if they are not there, you can search more broadly. You may not find any categories that match exactly. In that case, try to find two or three that combine to match your business. For example, if you have a home-based makeup business, you can use the combination of "Home Business", "Health/Beauty", and "Makeup Artist".

Bio - This is a short description of your business that will show right underneath your page name. Keep it short and descriptive (around 100 characters). You want to explain what you do in a sentence or two. This is a great place to put the slogan you may have wanted to put in the page name section. Don't worry, you will be able to enter a much longer description in the "About" section". When you are done with the bio, click Create and move on to the next section.

Congrats, you now have an "official" Facebook business page. I keep putting the word official in quotes because these three steps you just took to create the page are only the three things that are required to have Facebook render the page. There is still a lot to do if you want to have a business page that doesn't look like you have a seven-year-old as the CEO.

To help move your page past the kindergarten phase, Facebook will put you into their "setup wizard" to help complete the other important sections. These steps are very easy to complete but don't rush them. Make sure to take your time to fill out each section with as much information as possible. Facebook uses every piece of information it has to help match you with potential customers, so it's up to you how much you want to help that process. Here are some tips for the steps you will encounter.

Just like your personal profile, your business page cover photo and profile picture will be the main focus when people go to learn more about you. Let's talk strategy:

Profile Picture: Most often, businesses would put their logo here but if you are a single-operator business like a realtor or independent salesperson feel free to add your business headshot. Make sure you use a high-quality image; it should be clear and visible, not a mysterious blob.

Cover Photo: Here's where you can let your inner fashion photographer shine. Choose a photo that tells the story of your business. Maybe it's a shot of your office that looks like it's straight out of a magazine, your team looking like they're ready to save the world, or your fleet of trucks that appear more ready for a parade than a house call. Just remember, professionalism is key – no blurry, stretched, or pixelated pics. You want 'wow', not 'what?!'

And a word to the wise, don't just kidnap any old photo from the depths of the internet. That's a one-way ticket to getting your page banned. Make sure you have the rights to every picture you use on your page.

Lynnesight - If you don't have a logo or professional pictures of your business you can use a service like Canva.com to create them. Canva has hundreds of business templates for any type of creative asset you may need. I use Canva all the time and can attest to its ease of use and quality templates. They also have a library of stock images that are approved for use on your website and business material, so if you need images, Canva can do that too. There are a bunch of videos and content on the web for Canva as well, so if you need a tutorial or info on how to locate anything, you will be able to find that easily from a few Google searches.

Action Button - This is a super important feature for the success of your page. This action button is the main way you are going to have your current and potential customers contact you from your business page. There are 16 different actions you can customize to the action button, separated into 3 categories. Make sure you go through and select the right one for your business.

Inviting friends - Don't miss the chance to send your newly created Facebook business page to your friends list. This is a quick and easy way to help your business page get noticed. Just a warning, most users miss these notifications so don't get too upset if you don't get a ton of responses. The goal would be to get at least 100 likes/followers which opens up your page to advanced analytics and other options, but if you don't get them all right away don't worry as it will happen soon enough.

You are right at the midway point. You've created the page, gone through the initial wizard, and are ready to put the final touches to make your business page complete. But, before we do that, we have to take a quick pause to explain the differences between your newly created page profile and your personal Facebook profile.

Navigating between your Personal Profile and Business Page Profile on Facebook can be a maze, thanks to Facebook's decision to let users embody two personas. While your profile showcases friends and memories, your business persona lets you engage on the platform as your brand and update your business page content. To identify which profile you're using on a desktop, check the top right corner: your account photo means you're on your account, while your business logo or headshot indicates the business profile. On mobile, this indicator is bottom right. Always double-check before posting or interacting to ensure you're using the proper profile. You may need to switch back and forth to edit your business page and access features that are not usable with a personal profile.

Before we go into filling your business page with posts, there are a few more important things you should do to make sure that your page is the best it can be. I am not going to go into blow-by-blow details on exactly how these additional things are done. If I did, this book would have to come with its four-wheeled carrying case. This part of the business page setup is optional, just because it is optional does not mean it's unimportant. The more you put into these things, the more you will get out of them. I also have an entire course on "Creating a Facebook Business Page that Converts" that you can check out on the website www.zuckmylife.com. If you are serious about having a great business page and want to see video instructions on how to do everything in this chapter, I would highly recommend checking that out.

To dive into the page settings, click "Manage Page" and then "Settings". This takes you to "General Page Settings". The most important thing to do here is to update your "Username". Doing this will change the URL of your page from a jumbled number to a brand-consistent word or phrase. See example below:

"https://www.facebook.com/profile.php?id=123456789" to "https://www.facebook.com/coolbusinessname".

In "Privacy", you can adjust settings for content visibility, restrictions, and interactions. Don't be too overwhelmed with the amount of settings in the menu. I think Facebook has a setting for each lawsuit they've faced!

Under "New Pages Experience" you can manage page access. This is important because you should always have a backup administrator, be it a trusted coworker or family member, to avoid losing access to your page if something were to happen to your profile. When you create the page, your profile is added as an admin by default, but we have seen situations where clients have lost business pages that have had years of posts, reviews, and engagement because they did not have a backup admin. FYI, when I say admin I mean "Facebook Access". In Facebook business page settings, what used to be called "admin" access is now called "Facebook Access" because why not change something that people know and understand, to something that makes absolutely no sense? "Facebook Access" on a business page means you have access to all functionality of the page, you know, like an admin (insert eye roll).

The last few important settings to understand are "Notifications" and "Linked Accounts". The "Notifications" settings centralize your alert preferences, while "Linked Accounts" is crucial for connecting your business's Instagram for shared posts, insights, and more. Alright, alright, alright intrepid Facebook adventurers (extra points if you just read that in Matthew McConaughey's voice). We've birthed our business page, added all the information we could, and are now ready to set out into the real and scary world of public Facebook posting. This is the moment when we turn our empty business page into a vibrant village of virtual value! My 5th-grade English teacher would be so proud of my alliteration skills.

I've found that one of the biggest hurdles for most small businesses when talking about posting on their Facebook business page is that they believe that there is a specific "something" they should be posting. Honestly, nothing could be further from the truth. There is no magic post type, subject, or format that you are "supposed" to use. What is important is that you utilize the three E's in every post you make. They are Entertain, Educate, and Engage. I am sure some of you are thinking, "I'd rather juggle, recite Shakespeare, and tap dance instead of thinking of how to do that in every post!" As much as I would like to take you up on your offer and watch you do that, I'll break it down so it's not so intimidating.

The first of our three E's is Entertain. I hope that by now you can see the value of entertaining an audience when talking about a subject that may not be so interesting otherwise (wink, wink). Just look at the ads during the Super Bowl. Over the last 3 years, the average cost of a Super Bowl ad was about 6 Million dollars for just 30 seconds. Given the high cost and short amount of time you have to make an impression on the audience, why do you think most brands opt for a funny way to feature their brand? It's because when you stimulate emotion with your content, it immediately becomes more memorable. Now I know that you are not Doritos and you aren't trying to sell your product to hundreds of millions of people, but the concept is the same just on a much smaller scale. You only have one chance to make a good first impression, so don't miss that opportunity! Think of ways your content can make people smirk, laugh out loud, or be so funny they share with their friends. Has anyone ever sent you a link and said, "You have to check out this boring ad on YouTube?" Just remember to walk a fine line. Keep your humor free of cringe and controversy. Think dad jokes vs. locker room jokes.

The second E is Educate. As the business owner, you are the most knowledgeable person on your product or service, but your potential customer is not. Don't miss the opportunity to educate people while you feature what you do. Just like laughter, when you are the one teaching someone about something they don't already know, they will associate you (and your business) with what they have learned and call you when they need it. You are teaching people the importance of brushing their teeth, so you can sell them toothpaste.

The last E is Engage. One of the biggest advantages of being on Facebook is the ability to interact with your audience and have them interact with you. You can't comment on a Billboard unless you are willing to climb up there and spray-paint your thoughts. I mean, you physically can but that is very dangerous, illegal, and usually reserved for teenage boys. Even though the capability is there, no one is going to engage with your content unless it compels people to do so. Think dialogues not monologues. If you go on a date and the other person just spends the whole time talking about themselves, what they do, what they have accomplished, and how great they are…How does that feel? Instead of vomiting information about your products and services all the time, take advantage of the medium you are using. Ask a question, post a poll, and encourage people to provide feedback. You would be shocked at how many people are scrolling through Facebook just waiting to interact with someone, anyone, even a business! If you do this, make sure to check back to respond, recognize, and react to engagement by your audience. The way you treat people on Facebook is a representation of how you will treat them as customers.

Lastly, make sure you add media to each post. Pictures, videos, emojis, and colored backgrounds are all great ways to make your content stand out. Don't think you need to hire a professional media crew to follow you around to make content for your page. You have everything you need right in your pocket. Grab your phone, take pictures, talk into the camera, and grab "real-life" content. The realer the better. People are not just buying your product or service, they are buying you. So make sure that you feature yourself along with your content for the best results.

Lynnesight - Don't overthink your first few posts. You should get about 5 posts created right away so your page looks current. You can use Canva.com to create media for page posts too. You can take a regular picture with a few sentences to place in a pre-built Canva template, which takes only a few minutes, but will add a few pretty posts for your new page. You can even use some of the Facebook default backgrounds and colors to spruce up a simple post. So the overall theme is that the posts you do in the beginning don't have to be elaborate or follow the three E's, but if you have ideas and media, go for it.

Questions: Post Your Answers in our Free group at facebook.com/groups/fbinsta101

Did you create a new Facebook Business Page? We'd love it if you'd post it in the group so we can see your great work.

Did you have an existing Facebook Business Page and use this chapter to improve it? We would love for you to post as well.

Was there a particular part of the Facebook Business page setup that was difficult or confusing?

<u>**Key Takeaways:**</u>

Fill out all the information you can on your business page, the more info the better

Only use good photos - professional photos, stock images, or pictures taken with a good phone or camera

Make sure your page has a decent amount of content, try to use the three E's method

Chapter 4:
When the Zuck will I start advertising?

Ah, the thrilling sensation of new beginnings! There you are, fresh-faced and brimming with optimism, having meticulously crafted what feels like the Sistine Chapel of Facebook Business Pages. Every detail, from the cover photo to the succinct bio, has been polished to perfection. You've imagined the hordes of new customers flocking to your page, each click a symphony, each like a standing ovation. You wonder, should I make room in my garage for three Ferraris?

But, as the seconds turn to minutes and the minutes become hours, the grim reality sets in. The vast digital arena of possibility seems eerily silent. The only sound? The mocking chirps of digital crickets and the faint echo of your once soaring expectations plummeting. A nagging question begins to loop in your mind, growing louder with each passing moment, "I built it, poured my soul into it... so why, oh why, aren't they storming in?!"

As much as Kevin Costner wants you to believe that "If you build it, they will come", rarely does it ever work right away on Facebook. This doesn't mean that you just wasted your time building an amazing business page, that was and is necessary, but if you want to skip the waiting and get more eyeballs on your content you are going to have to find a way to get a boost.

There are about 4.75 billion items shared by Facebook users each day. Let that sink in for a second. With so much user-generated content floating around each day, it is no wonder that only a few people are seeing your business page posts. Luckily, Facebook is a for-profit company and would gladly exchange greater reach into their user's content feeds in exchange for money. Also, it certainly helps offset the cost of keeping a utility used by half the planet, free of charge for users. Welcome to the world of Facebook Advertising, queue the royal trumpets!

Let me explain why I used the word "World" when describing Facebook Advertising. It is quite literally a whole new world (a new fantastic point of view) sorry, couldn't help it. A more accurate description would be an undiscovered digital jungle. If you have attempted to try and advertise on your own, you probably felt like you had been dropped in by a helicopter with just a loincloth and a pocket dictionary. You were suddenly expected to decipher cryptic language like algorithms, conversion APIs, and pixel tracking. You timidly tiptoed around terms like 'Lookalike Audiences' and 'Ad Sets,' and you probably had the feeling that you crash-landed into an episode of "Star Trek." But instead of being the captain or main crew, you were the red-shirt guy who didn't even have a name and was the first to die when something went wrong. It's no wonder that many think of Facebook advertising as the Bermuda Triangle of the business world…where marketing budgets and sanity disappear.

For those of you that have tried advertising on Facebook and failed, I see you. Most small businesses that have become successful running Facebook ads did it by failing upwards. Fortunately, I had the privilege of seeing through the digital jungle while working at Facebook. The most important lesson I learned is going to sound disappointing. There isn't a secret door, special weapon, or unknown path that leads to success. It is just good old-fashioned education, explanation, and experimentation. In this chapter, I will show you the different advertising entry points (AKA places where you can create ads on Facebook) and their capability. Some of the terminology used in the features of these entry points may be unfamiliar, but rest assured, we will explain these in detail in the following chapter.

The Boost Button - Your First Dance with Facebook Ads

I am sure by now you have seen that big blue button that says "Boost Post" under all of the content you posted on your business page. If you did not see it, there may be a digital designer in Menlo Park, CA who will be receiving a really bad performance review. The good thing is that Facebook is not clueless about the plight of small business advertisers. They know how difficult and complex their advertising system is, but after a decade of development and hundreds of millions of customers using the current system, it is hard to make wholesale changes to make it easier without a complete rebuild of their system. In simple terms, they need to do their best with what they have. That is why products like the Boost button have been developed. The Boost button is Facebook's version of Staples' "Easy Button". They know that there is a big barrier to entry into the world of Facebook Ads, so they had to find a way to make it so easy to get started, that anyone would give it a try.

Boosted posts are essentially Facebook ads wearing a wig, fake mustache, and sunglasses. Many small business advertisers don't even know that boosting is advertising. When you boost, your original post is turned into an ad and you are given a limited list of options on how you can promote the post. For users new to advertising and don't have any clue where to start, this is great. They can get their posts out to user's feeds that may not have ever seen their content before. But what you may not know is just how limited the boost post option is. As we go through the rest of this book you will see how much more control and power you get when you opt to use more advanced methods of advertising. The best a boosted post can do is target specific genders, ages, locations, and some detailed targeting like demographics, interests, and behaviors. That's it. You set your budget, and timeframe and enter a payment method and you are off and running. The main point of boosting is to show your post to more people and you can define some of the characteristics of who they are. As you will see as you go further into this book this bare minimum approach, while easy, is not very effective.

While I don't completely dismiss the idea of boosting posts (they've genuinely benefited some of my small business clients), fans of boosting posts may not realize its limited scope. Imagine being handed a car, and you think, "Great! This beats walking!" But then you realize the car barely hits 10 MPH, can't make turns, and is afraid of the dark. Sure, it works, but if someone then offered you a fully-equipped car with all available features, you'd be tempted to send that first car off the edge of a cliff, right? By diving into this book, you're showing me you're after more than just a one-button solution. Let's ensure you're not cruising in a lemon.

Facebook certainly doesn't hide the fact that they offer advertising. It's like walking through a candy store with samples lurking at every corner. Instead of candy bars, it's the sweet temptation of advertising. Create a post? Why not boost it? Did you share a picture? Let's promote it! Just get a new customer? How about letting the whole world see it for just a few bucks? It's as if every nook and cranny of the platform winks at businesses, whispering, "Go on, just one little ad won't hurt." The ads growth team must have taken a page out of Willy Wonka's playbook, turning Facebook into a world of pure advertising temptation!

We've already covered the idea of the boosted post, our first window into the world of Facebook advertising. But, there are three more ways to get started, each with its unique interface and set of features. You can create ads from your Business Page, or utilize Meta's Business Suite, or Ads Manager. We will review all of them, but the one we will be covering in depth, and what we recommend you use is Ads Manager. Ads Manager has all the features and functionality available to advertisers on Facebook &

Instagram is also the most complex and complicated to use. But don't worry, we will explain everything so it is easy for you to understand.

The first major advertising entry point is creating an ad from your Facebook Business Page. If you want to see what this looks like, go to your Facebook business page, spot the "Create Ads" option in the "Manage Page" menu, and click. This opens up an interface that looks a lot like the boost menu but with a few added frills. This ad entry point retains all the boost features, but it also lets you set a goal and change / improve your creative components like images and copy. An improvement, and a decent place to advertise if you are running one ad campaign, but the greatest strength of Facebook ads is in the many features you can use, and this option removes a lot of them.

The second major entry point is through a product called the Meta Business Suite. Now, before we get into how MBS is connected to advertising, I just want to let you know how much I love this product. Some days I spend hours just staring up at the Meta Business Suite poster I got from last November's Teen Beat magazine…so dreamy. In all seriousness, this is a Facebook business product that I believe doesn't get enough credit, use, or promotion. There is so much you can do with this tool. The business suite is an all-in-one business platform that consolidates your organic and paid efforts for Facebook and Instagram in a single view. You can create any type of content, schedule content delivery, see insights on your page or IG account, and see all your messages for both Messenger and Instagram in one view. If you have an active business page and IG account, you should check out Meta Business Suite. To access this free tool you must have an existing business page. You can get to the product by simply typing business.facebook.com into a browser and it will appear. Beyond being a great place to see a consolidated view of your organic accounts, the business suite has a leads center that stores leads from any forms you are running on Facebook as well as a built-in CRM where you can keep customer notes, track status, and sales…all for free. I may just write my next book on this.

If you click to create an ad through MBS you will see a view that is virtually identical to the ad builder from your Facebook business page. The only changes are the ability to choose some ready-made custom audiences (which we discuss later) for people who like your page, or who are similar to people who like your page. This and the Facebook page ad interface are meant to be simple starting points for single-campaign small business advertisers.

The final product we will introduce in this chapter is Ads Manager. Ads Manager is the most robust, feature-rich, and effective ad system that Meta has to offer. But it comes with a small catch…It is ridiculously complicated. Imagine that the Facebook Page and Business Suite ad interfaces are like a bicycle, Ads Manager is a space shuttle. The bicycle is straightforward, easy to understand, and takes you from point A to B without any frills. On the other hand, the space shuttle has countless controls, and advanced features, and can take you to another planet, but requires extensive knowledge and expertise to operate. You can get to the ads manager at facebook.com/adsmanager. You can explore if you'd like, but the next 5 chapters will be dedicated to helping you understand what you need to know to use Facebook Ads Manager and get started with your first campaign. So, buckle up this is when things start to get good.

How do you feel about the potential complexity of Facebook advertising?

Have you used any method of advertising on Facebook or Instagram? Let us know which one and what you thought about the experience.

<u>Key Takeaways:</u>

The only way to get your content out to a big audience consistently is by advertising

Boosting posts is a type of advertising that leaves out most of the best functionalities available on Facebook, but is easy

There are multiple interfaces you can use to advertise: Your business page, Meta Business Suite, and Ads Manager

Chapter 5:
It's Not Personal, It's Strictly Business Ad Accounts

A Facebook ad account is like the engine under the hood of your car. While you might marvel at the sleek body style and the comfortable modern interior, it's the engine (the ad account) that powers the whole thing, propelling it forward and ensuring it responds precisely to your commands. But just like an engine, ad accounts require regular maintenance, fine-tuning, and a clear understanding of its intricacies to ensure smooth and optimal performance. If neglected, it can sputter, stall, or even come to a complete halt. So, while the shiny ads might get all the attention, it's the ad account that's the MVP behind the scenes.

A personal ad account, typically linked to an individual's Facebook profile, is intended for personal use or for businesses just starting to explore the world of Facebook ads. It offers basic features and is directly managed through a personal Facebook account. However, when it comes to scaling up your advertising efforts, a business ad account using Meta Business Manager becomes a better choice. This type of account is tailored for larger businesses or those requiring more sophisticated advertising tools. It provides advanced features such as detailed analytics, team collaboration options, and better control over ad spending and user permissions. Additionally, a business ad account ensures a clear separation between personal and professional activities, offering enhanced security and privacy. This differentiation is key in developing an effective Facebook advertising strategy, as it aligns your ad management capabilities with your business's evolving needs.

Everyone who has a personal profile on Facebook has (or will have) their ad account. If you don't have one already, an ad account is created instantaneously when you access any of Facebook's Advertising entry points. If you navigate to Ads Manager at adsmanager.facebook.com, you can see your ad account appear at the top of the page. It could / should show your name followed by several digits (your ad account ID). While you can run ads from a personal ad account, it is not recommended. Just like you wouldn't use your funds to run your business, you don't want your ad account to operate your business ads. Instead, you should open a Facebook Business Account. Here is where things get a little confusing and complex. To create a Business Account, you have to first create a Business Manager.

Meta Business Manager is designed to streamline and simplify the management of your business. You can set up a Business Account within the business manager to consolidate business assets, like business pages and Instagram accounts, as well as maintain your privacy on Facebook. Because Facebook personal and business profiles are so intertwined, if you want to keep your personal Facebook profile private from people you work with, you must have and use a business account. If you advertise using your ad account, and you want to invite others to have access, you will need to be friends with them to do so. Some people do not want to share their info with business colleagues or freelancers who may be helping them with Facebook business activities which is why the Business Account was created. If you invite people to work inside your business account, they will only see your name, work email, and the specific Pages and ad accounts you manage. This separation ensures your personal Facebook profile remains private, while you oversee business operations.

Just leave it to Facebook to create the most complicated and confusing way to do business on their platform. This again all stems back to the fact that Facebook was originally developed as a way for people to connect personally, and then the business part was added on using thumbtacks and duct tape. Then when new features needed to be added, they were added with glue and paper clips. So now we have a system that takes in Billions of dollars that is essentially computer code spaghetti. Which explains a lot when you think about it.

Besides privacy, which is usually not an entrepreneur or small business's main complaint, the biggest perk of a Business Account is the ability to create ad accounts on demand. When you create an ad account from a Business Account, it is completely separated from your profile.

To set up a Business Account go to business.facebook.com/overview and click "Create account". There you will enter your business name, your name and work email address, and your business details. Once the account is set up you can add people, Business Pages, Instagram accounts, and create ad accounts so you can manage all your assets in one place.

The front-end access to your business account is the Meta Business Suite, which I mentioned earlier (well not just mentioned I was swooning over it). Once your business account is created you can go to business.facebook.com to access that platform. I highly recommend you use Business Accounts and Meta Business Suite if you are serious about growing your business with Meta. The tools, access, analytics, and features (all free by the way) are critical to your overall success.

OK, now that the super confusing explanation of personal ad accounts vs. business accounts is over, we can move on to explaining the inner workings of an ad account and how to use it.

If you are using a personal or business ad account your settings will be in the "ad account settings" section of the ads manager. You can get there by looking at the menu on the left and clicking the second to last icon that looks like two small tiles.

Right off the bat, you will need to do two things to make sure your ad account is ready to advertise. First, you need to confirm that you have Advertiser access or Facebook access to the Facebook Business Page where you would like to run ads. For most of you, since you created the page yourself, you should have this access automatically. If you did not set up the page or are advertising on someone's behalf, check to make sure you have "Facebook" access (which is essentially what everyone else calls admin access) or "advertiser" access. These can be found in the "New Pages Experience" section of the privacy menu for the business page.

The second thing you need to do is enter a payment method. Second only to the Gambino Family, Facebook cares a lot about collecting money for advertising. If you don't have a payment method set up already, you should see an alert on your ad account dashboard to enter a payment method. You can access the "payments" section of your ad account by going to the stacked coins icon on the left menu to go to the billing section. To pay for your ads you can use a credit card, PayPal, or bank account as payment methods. If your ad account is new and you have never advertised before, be aware that Facebook will charge your payment method in very small increments until you build up some history with them. You may see charges as low as $5, $10, or $15 until they know your card is good or you have the money to cover the balance. To see all settings available in your ad account you can go to "Ad account settings" in the Ads Manager menu, but as long as you have a payment method and proper access to a business page, you are ready to go.

You can explore the other settings in the ad account by clicking through the menu, but most are either self-explanatory or for more advanced advertisers

Lynnesight: I know all of this sounds overwhelming, but once you get it all built up and get a proper foundation it will make so much more sense. If someone handed you a book on basketball, you would know, recognize, and understand the game, but it wouldn't make sense until you played. That is the same with Facebook & Instagram Ads. You can understand all the terms, accounts, levels, settings, etc. and they are important to know, but the full understanding of how it works will only come when you start using it.

<u>Questions:</u> Post Your Answers in our Free group at <u>facebook.com/groups/fbinsta101</u>

Did you have any difficulties finding or understanding any of the ad account settings? If so, post and let us know.

Are you sure about what kind of ad account you would like to use? Post if you are still confused.

<u>**Key Takeaways:**</u>

Every Facebook personal profile has an ad account attached to it, you may have already used it for boosting posts or promoting marketplace listings

Personal ad accounts should not be used for business advertising in the long run

You can Create a Meta Business Manager account with a new ad account that will be associated with your business, not your profile

Chapter 6: Campaigns, Ad Sets, and Ads: The Three Zucketeers of Your Ad Account

Before we start building campaigns, we need to understand a few things about how ad campaigns are structured on Facebook. There are three main levels to a Facebook ad campaign: The campaign level, ad set level, and ad level. Because you most likely never heard of these terms before, it may be hard to understand the way this structure works. For me, I like to think of it like building a house. If you have ever purchased a new construction home, or seen one built on TV, you understand the "phases" that go into the home building process. There is the planning/blueprint phase, the infrastructure/construction phase, and the interior design phase. In the home build process, It is important to go in this particular order because if you don't plan properly in the beginning it will be too late if you want to add something later after construction is complete. You can't just wait until you move in to decide if you want a double sink vanity in your master bathroom because if the bathroom is already built the walls could be too narrow or there may not be enough plumbing to do what you want to do. These things you could have corrected if you thought of them earlier in the planning process. Just like building a home, your Facebook ad campaign needs to be carefully planned out in a particular order for it to work for your business. In the next section, we will explain what each level or Phase means, and explain the different inputs and options for each.

I know I said I'd try to keep this book fun and light, but sometimes, to get the hang of things, we have to get a bit serious. And this chapter is one of those times. It's super important that you understand how an ad account is set up and what all the different parts and settings do. So, for this chapter, I had to dial down the jokes and pack in more of the serious stuff.

I get it, this might not be the most thrilling stuff. So, if you're feeling a little sleepy, now's a good time to perk up. Maybe grab a cup of your favorite coffee, do a few jumping jacks, or even give yourself a little face slap. Do whatever works to keep you awake and focused. Trust me, you'll want to pay attention to this part. We're about to dive into some really important stuff that's going to help you a lot with your ads. So get ready, stay sharp, and let's get into the nitty-gritty of ad accounts.

The campaign level - Phase 1

When you set up your first ad campaign the first thing you will see is a pop-up box that contains options for buying type and campaign objective. We can keep the buying type as "auction" as that is what you want to use in 99.5% of all small business scenarios. There is another option called "reach and frequency" but that is used mostly for branding so we will not spend too much time talking about that as branding is not what most small businesses are looking for. These businesses want to get leads, make sales, and grow their business. Branding is certainly a part of the business plan, but it is hard to spend money on branding when you have no customers.

Campaign objectives are one of the most important things to understand if you want to create ads that deliver results. Facebook uses your campaign objective selection to deliver ads to the users that are most likely to fulfill your campaign objective. Pretty cool, right? But, what's not cool is that if you choose an objective that does not align with your ultimate goal, you could be targeting the wrong users which will lead to poor performance. Facebook considers it a win when the campaign fulfills its goal, not when your business makes money. That is why it is so important to select the right one. So take a deep breath and get ready to absorb this information. Let's review the six campaign options.

Awareness - The sole purpose of this objective is to bring awareness to your business. It's designed to find the maximum number of people who'll not just see but recall your ad. Like making a memorable first impression at a party, but digitally! If you are concerned about people knowing your business exists, then this is the way to go. For our clients who are trying to acquire leads, customers, and sales, this objective is often a secondary metric. They are trying to get people to know who they are, but you can achieve that while also trying to acquire them as customers. There are some exceptions. If you are promoting an event, non-profit organization, physical store location, or a new product, the use of the awareness campaign objective could be very helpful. It all depends on what you want for your business.

Traffic - The traffic objective aims to direct individuals to a target location, such as a website or an app. In a campaign using the traffic objective, Facebook is looking for "clickers", people who are more likely to click on ads they see in their Facebook feed, but that does not always mean they are the ones most likely to also buy your product. That is an important distinction to make. This objective is by far the most popular objective used by small businesses, but I do not believe it is always the right objective. I've heard statistics that say around 90% of small businesses only use the traffic objective. I am not saying to stop using the traffic objective together, but if almost every business is targeting "clickers" because they are all using the same ad objective, who is targeting people who don't click on ads? What about the people who message businesses directly, call them, watch videos, or look to research social media accounts…Who is targeting those potential clients?

Engagement - Engagement campaigns look to deliver your ads to users who are likely to message your business directly, call, or interact with your ad with likes and comments. If you are looking to get more conversations, video views, post engagement, and be an active participant with your potential client, then this is the right objective for your business. If you have a business that deals with immediacy, like most home services, people do not want to go to a website, fill out a form, and wait for a call. If you have a pipe that is leaking or ants all over your floor, the last thing you want to do is make people go through a three-step process to get in touch with you. With an engagement campaign, they can click to call or click to message and start an immediate conversation with you about the product or service. In any business, people have questions. In this scenario, you are inviting people to ask them directly, which is a great tool if used properly. This is a great way to showcase your customer service (if you have great customer service *wink*). Also, using this objective gets you out of the 90% target "clickers", and puts you into the feeds of people actively looking to talk to businesses, which could be a much better-performing audience for your business. Sounds great right? Before you get too excited, understand that this objective requires businesses to be active participants in social media, not passive ones. If you are sending traffic to your site, users do not expect that you will be there to answer their questions. If you use the engagement campaign objective, you are essentially telling users that you want to talk to them right now and that you are there to have that conversation. If you do not fulfill that expectation, you are giving a bad first impression to your potential clients. On the other hand, if you are attentive and fast to respond and answer questions, you set a different example. If someone takes 2 days to answer a Facebook message, do you believe they will show up at your house on time for an appointment? Do you believe that they are so organized that they will complete your project in the time they promised? Those are the conclusions your potential clients will draw if you have an engagement ad and you do not answer quickly. On the flip side, if you answer quickly and give clients what they are looking for, they may not hesitate to buy your product or service because they know they can communicate with you about any issues.

Leads - The lead objective allows users to tell businesses they are interested in their service and provide contact information. Here, Facebook will target users who are more likely to fill out a form or go through a qualifying sequence through Messenger. The lead objective is a good way to get closer to the engagement objective, but don't have the time or staff to answer messages and calls all day. The great thing about leads is that you are setting the expectation that you are not going to get back to them right away (but you should still try). If you use the lead objective, you will also unlock the leads section of Facebook Business Manager, where you can use that free tool to track all your leads if you are not already using a CRM.

App Promotion - Using app promotion ads allows you to find and deliver ads to people who are looking for and have a high likelihood of downloading an app directly from your ad. This is great for businesses who have an app, but most of our clients or even small businesses in general do not. But, if you do, this is the way to go.

Sales - The sales objective is looking for shoppers. People buy products directly from Facebook Instagram or other websites. If you have a product that you can sell directly through Meta and deliver to the buyer, this is a great way to cut out the extra steps of going to an e-commerce process or website. Using this objective opens up new ad units and targeting algorithms that are specifically designed for e-commerce. If you are selling a physical product, you must start using the sales objective. To use the sales objective to sell directly from your ad you will need to build a Facebook or Instagram Shop. The other option is to integrate your e-commerce platform with Facebook. As of the writing of this book, Facebook integrates with 11 of the biggest e-commerce platforms including Shopify, WooCommerce, Magento, OpenCart, and, more. One of the biggest advances in Facebook advertising over the last few years is the development of an algorithm called Advantage+ Shopping Campaigns or ASC. Advantage+ Shopping Campaigns are a component of Meta's Advantage+ suite, harnessing machine learning to efficiently connect your products with high-value audiences. With a focus on performance, this tool is tailor-made for advertisers aiming to boost online sales. When compared with traditional manual shopping ads, the Advantage+ approach stands out. It minimizes the steps in campaign creation, refines audience selection, and simplifies the creative. If you have a product that is sold via a website, you can and should still use the sales objective. The only difference between using a website vs a Facebook or Instagram shop is that you will need to install additional tracking methods on your site, like Facebook Pixel and Conversion API, to ensure that Meta can see and track purchases made outside their platform.

Other than selecting a campaign objective, there are a few other settings that sit on the campaign level. They are the Special Ad category, A/B Testing, and Advantage campaign budget. It is hard to understand these options without a greater understanding of the other two phases in the campaign, so we explain them at the end of this chapter.

The Ad Set Level - Phase 2

Now that you understand the type of campaigns available we are ready to move on to phase 2 which is the ad set level. You have to create at least one ad set in a campaign but you can have as many ad sets as you want. Ad sets are groups or containers used for your ads so that they can share common settings. Since we just began learning about all the settings available in Ads Manager, it is hard to appreciate a functionality that will allow you to share settings, but believe me when I say that it is an amazing feature. The settings they can share could be conversion location, performance goal, audience targeting, budgeting, and ad placements.

Ad sets could be one of the more confusing segments of Facebook ads, so I want to make sure that it is crystal clear what they are and how they are used. Where the campaign level focuses more on the overall "what and why" of your Facebook ads like traffic or sales, the ad set level works on the "where and who" of your ads. The "where" covers the destination of your ad, like a website, and the "who" covers the type of person you want your ad to target using things like age, gender, location, and interests. Because you can have multiple ad sets, you can create numerous segments of "wheres and whos" within one campaign. For example, if you were a photography coach, you could create a traffic campaign that has two ad sets. The first could target 18-24-year-olds interested in photography and send people to your Instagram profile to build your following. The other ad set could send 25-45-year-olds to your website to see your coaching packages. Remember, you can mix and match the audiences and locations with different ad sets, but you always have to use the same campaign objective which in this case is traffic (sending users to a location).

While most of the settings are somewhat self-explanatory like audience, location, and budget, I want to take a second to explain performance goals. If you remember from our campaign-level explanation, defining the campaign's purpose helps the platform determine the type of user to show your ad. For example, people who click a lot of ads will be shown traffic campaigns and people who like and comment will be shown more engagement ads. The performance goal setting in the ad set helps Facebook understand what particular action you would like to define as success, so it can try to get you more. These goals, or actions on Facebook, vary from campaign to campaign but can lead to huge differences in your performance. For example, within the traffic campaign, if you were sending traffic to a website, you can choose a goal of link clicks or landing page views in the ad set. If you choose clicks, then Facebook will consider your campaign better or more successful if people simply click a link on your ad. But, if you choose landing page views, Facebook will try to optimize not just for clicks of links on your ads, but for clicks from people who made it to your website and saw information. Do you see the distinction here? If you choose landing page views as the goal vs clicks, then Facebook will try to get you more of the clicks that led to your site content vs the ones who just clicked your ad to see more information, your business page, or any other clickable element.

Some performance goals are not hard to understand because they are common actions people take on Facebook like link clicks, clicks to messages, or video views. Some others use marketing terms but are easy enough to explain like Impressions (how many times the ad is shown), reach (how many different people see the ad), and conversations (how many people started messaging you). Then other goals are not actions people take on Facebook, but ones that take place on your website. Those include conversions, conversion value, leads, landing page views, and purchases. Now you may be asking yourself, how can Facebook know if someone went to my website and performed a goal? Well, they actually can't, unless you are using Facebook Pixel tracking.

The Facebook pixel is a powerful tool you can add to your website that aids in measuring, refining, and creating target audiences for your advertising campaigns. Think of it as a sophisticated mini-program that gauges the success of your ads by tracking users' behaviors on your site.

The biggest benefit to using the Facebook pixel is that you are giving Facebook a view into the type of people that visit your website and allow them to use that information to improve your advertising campaigns. Using the pixel, you can do things like to create custom audiences, target users who are likely to take action on your website and be able to report the results of your advertising efforts. Upon installation on your website or funnel, the pixel activates whenever someone interacts with your site. These interactions, or "events", are then reflected in your Facebook pixel page within the Events Manager. This grants you a view into your audience's behaviors and the opportunity to reconnect with them using future Facebook ads. We will be going over this in more detail when we talk about tracking and reporting.

The Ad - Phase 3

This is the phase that you will be most familiar with because you probably see (depending on how many hours a day you spend on Facebook) tens to hundreds of Facebook Ads. The different types of ads are called "formats". There are four major ad formats. Image ads that feature high-quality and engaging digital visuals. Video Ads that feature videos to help promote your products through sound and motion. Carousel Ads, which can display up to ten images or videos within a single ad. And finally, Collection Ads encourage users to shop by displaying items from a product catalog. Most small businesses use the image and video formats, so we will stick to those going forward.

A Facebook ad consists of the ad "creative" which can be an image or video. Next, you will need ad copy and headline, which are the written words that will show along with the image or video creative. And finally a call to action button, which contains the user destination and tracking.

First, let's talk about ad creativity. The most important part of the ad is the image or video section. This is the section of the ad that will need to grab the user's attention and "stop the scroll". There are a few things to consider when choosing an image for your ad. Only use the highest quality images. If you do not have high-quality images of your business, you can search for stock images online or use a tool like Canva to create an image using a template. Make sure you steer clear of excessively edited photos. Be sure to feature your brand or logo on the image. Show people that resemble your target market using your product or service if at all possible. This encourages viewers to envision themselves using your product or service. For example, If you are targeting moms, show a woman carrying a baby, pushing a stroller, or having toys in the room to show the user that the person in the ad is a mother. I would strongly suggest using text overlays in the image. Make sure the text doesn't distract from the image itself, but this is a great way to use text formats you cannot replicate through ad copy or the headline. You can use big text, different fonts, colors, and other text edits to make your ad stand out. Don't waste any space in the image either, make sure you choose something that uses the maximum amount of space displaying your product or service. You only have a few seconds to get the user's attention so it is so important to be as efficient as possible with your resources.

Using video is a great way to get high engagement with your ad. I have yet to see a still picture creative that was able to get more engagement than a video, so I strongly suggest you add at least one video ad to all of your ad sets. Capture interest within the initial three seconds. With fleeting attention spans, it's crucial to engage viewers immediately. Achieve this with a captivating thumbnail, a compelling slogan, or a strong opening statement. Ensuring early engagement increases the likelihood of viewership until the end, leading to potential conversions. Opt for vertical videos. This format is favored on social media, aligning with user expectations and viewing habits. Keep it concise. While longer videos can deter viewers, shorter ones often boast higher completion rates. Aim for a 30-second runtime to maintain viewer engagement without overwhelming or irritating them. Although there are instances where extended durations are warranted, it's best to keep it short and sweet. Given that videos default to silent autoplay, they should be understandable without sound. Given the likelihood of users scrolling past muted videos, subtitles are essential. Without them, the message may be lost to those who prefer silent viewing. Prioritize authenticity. Genuine content resonates more than polished, overproduced videos. Some of the most impactful ads arise from business owners candidly discussing their offerings via simple phone recordings. Evoke emotion. Ads that stir feelings, especially positive ones, enhance brand recall and content retention. Research indicates that emotionally charged ads outperform neutral ones nearly twofold. Integrate social proof. Our purchasing decisions often lean on others' endorsements. Capitalize on this by weaving in customer testimonials, accolades, or reviews. These elements not only foster trust but can also elevate your click-through rate.

Lynnesight: Auto-generated subtitles are created when you upload a video to Facebook for use in your ad. But other options look a little better and are more recognizable to users who consume a lot of video content online. You can use an app to easily transcribe and automatically apply captions that you can customize using size, location, animations, and colors. These captions are much better than the auto-generated options and will help get your videos more engaged. There are many apps to do this, but the one we recommend is called "Captions".

Ad copy is the text portion of your Facebook ad. It's where you tell your story, explain your offer, or describe your product or service. Good ad copy resonates with the audience, reflects your brand's voice, and is tailored to the specific goal of your campaign, whether that's driving sales, increasing website visits, or boosting engagement. Ad copy is not just text; it's the narrative force of your Facebook ad, the persuasive element that can turn a casual browser into a committed customer. This textual component is where the magic of your marketing happens – it's storytelling, it's selling, and it's engaging, all rolled into one. In our experience, the best ad copy hits the pain points that your product or service solves in the first few sentences. Facebook will only show a small portion of the ad copy and hide the rest allowing the user to expand the copy by clicking "see more". It is best practice to keep the most important parts of your copy above the "see more" cutoff which you can see in the preview portion when setting up the ad in the ads manager.

The headline is arguably the most critical part of your Facebook ad. It's the first line of text that appears below your image or video and acts as a hook to draw people in. An effective headline makes the difference between someone stopping to read your ad or scrolling past it. The headline of your Facebook ad holds immense power, much like the first impression on a first date. It's the gateway to your ad goal, the make-or-break moment that decides whether a user will pause their scroll to engage with what you have to say. This small but mighty line of text below your image or video is much more than just a few words; it's your ad's opening act, its handshake, and its eye contact with the audience. Like the first few lines of the ad copy, it is important to use the most compelling part of your offer in the ad headline as you only have 40 characters of space.

A CTA (Call To Action) is a prompt or instruction within the ad that encourages the viewer to take a specific action. It is a clear directive telling the audience what step they should take next. The CTA is crucial because it guides potential customers toward the goal of your ad, whether it's making a purchase, signing up for a newsletter, downloading an app, or visiting a webpage. Without a clear CTA, even the most engaging and well-designed ad can fail to convert interest into action. Common CTAs in Facebook ads include "Shop Now," "Learn More," "Sign Up," "Download," and "Contact Us." These are usually presented as clickable buttons or links within the ad.

The destination refers to where the user ends up after clicking on your ad. This could be a specific page on your website, a landing page, an app download page, or any other place you want to direct your audience. The destination is where the conversion process continues or concludes. The destination needs to match the promise or offer in the ad. For instance, if the ad is for a specific product, the destination should be that product's purchase page, not your homepage. The relevance and alignment of the destination with the ad content are vital. If there's a disconnect between the ad and where the user lands after clicking, it can lead to confusion and a higher likelihood of the user leaving without taking further action.

Tracking Facebook ads involves collecting data on how users interact with your ad. This includes whether they clicked on it, how they engaged with it, and what actions they took afterward. Tracking is essential for understanding the effectiveness of your ad. It allows you to measure key performance indicators (KPIs) like click-through rates, conversion rates, and return on ad spend. This data is crucial for evaluating the success of your campaign and for making informed decisions on how to optimize future ads. Facebook provides tools like the Facebook Pixel and conversion tracking to help advertisers track user behavior. The Pixel, for instance, is a piece of code you place on your website that tracks visitors' actions after they click on your ad. This information helps you understand how well your ad is performing and whether it's achieving its intended goals. You can also append tracking values to the destination URL of your ad if you are using a third-party tracking solution like Google Analytics or others.

Facebook Budgeting

A Daily Budget is the average amount you're willing to spend on an ad set per day. Facebook will pace your spending per day, but the amount spent might vary slightly from day to day. However, over the length of the campaign, Facebook will average it out so you don't spend more than your daily budget times the number of days in your campaign.

A Lifetime Budget is the total amount you're willing to spend over the entire lifespan of your ad set or campaign. Facebook will optimize your spending across the entire period to get the best results based on your ad delivery settings.

Facebook offers tools and algorithms to help optimize your budget for the best results. For example, if you run multiple ad sets, Facebook can allocate more of your budget to the higher-performing sets.

Facebook uses pacing to ensure your budget is spent evenly over your campaign's scheduled time or to optimize spending for the best results throughout the day.

Lynnesight: If you are going to use multiple ad sets, I highly recommend setting the budget at the ad set level, especially in the beginning and during the testing phases. If you set it at the campaign level, it will optimize and allocate the money toward the better-performing ad sets automatically. This can be helpful once your campaign has been up and running for a while but initially, I feel it is more helpful to get data and metrics from the individual ad sets. If you set the budget at the ad set level you will have more control and can make optimizations more easily.

Billing

When you first start advertising on Facebook, you'll set up a payment method and initially have a low billing threshold. This threshold is the amount your ad spend can reach before you're billed. As you continue advertising and making successful payments, your billing threshold may increase. Billing frequency depends on how quickly your ad spend reaches your billing threshold or when you reach the end of your monthly bill date. You can pay for Facebook ads using various methods, such as credit cards, debit cards, PayPal, and others, depending on your country. You are charged for Facebook ads based on the amount of interaction your ads receive, like impressions or clicks, and how your campaigns are set up. The specific cost can be influenced by various factors including your bidding strategy, ad quality, and competition for ad space. Facebook provides invoices and receipts for your ad spending in the billing section of your Ads Manager. These documents detail the amount spent and can be used for accounting and tax purposes. Through the Ads Manager, you can monitor your spending in real-time. It's important to regularly check your ad spend to ensure it aligns with your marketing budget. You can adjust your budgets or pause campaigns at any time if you see that you're spending more than intended.

Ad Policies

Facebook's ad policies and guidelines are designed to ensure that ads are safe, respectful, and suitable for their diverse audience. Advertisers must comply with these policies to run ads on the platform. Here's an overview of some key aspects of these policies:

It is important to note that these are guidelines. In the end, it is Facebook who ultimately determines if your ad violates their policies according to how they interpret the content, which may be much different from your interpretation. To be safe, it is best to avoid anything that may be even remotely close to language or subject matter that could trigger one of these policies. Every time one of your ads gets flagged, that mark stays on your ad account so Facebook can keep track of advertisers who are trying to get around their policies. Just like your parents and teachers told you in High School, don't fall into the bad crowd. If you violate ad policy to a certain point, Facebook can disable your ad account temporarily or permanently. Here are a few of the most common policies that you may run into when advertising. Just know that Facebook can update, change, and interpret these as they see fit.

Safety and Respect: Ads must not contain content that is misleading, discriminatory, offensive, or promotes harmful behavior. This includes hate speech, harassment, or content that exploits or endangers individuals.

Illegal Products or Services: Ads must not promote products, services, or activities that are illegal in the location where the ad is displayed.

Discriminatory Practices: Ads must not discriminate against or marginalize individuals or groups.

Adult Content: Adult products, services, or content are generally prohibited.

Misleading or False Content: Deceptive practices, misleading claims, or false information are not allowed.

Dangerous Products or Services: The promotion of weapons, explosives, drugs, and tobacco products is prohibited.

Alcohol: Ads that promote alcohol must comply with local laws and target appropriate age demographics.

Dating Services: Dating ads are subject to additional guidelines and require prior permission.

Political and Social Issues: Ads about political topics or social issues may require authorization and must include a disclaimer.

Ads must not use targeting options to discriminate against, harass, provoke, or disparage users or engage in predatory advertising practices.

Ads should maintain a high level of quality, avoiding excessive use of capitalization, punctuation, and gimmicky language.

Landing pages linked from ads must be functional, relevant to the ad, and not deceptive in what they offer.

Ad positioning should not lead to a disruptive user experience. This includes considerations for where and how ads are displayed on the platform.

Advertisers must respect user privacy and data use policies. This includes not using sensitive personal data for ad targeting.

Practices designed to circumvent Facebook's review processes, such as cloaking or using other deceptive practices, are prohibited.

All ads undergo a review process to check their compliance with these policies. Ads that violate policies may be rejected. Advertisers can appeal decisions on ad rejection. Repeated violations can lead to account restrictions or bans.

Lynnesight: Believe me I know this is a lot of information. We do not expect you to retain the majority of information in this chapter the first time you read it. Hearing it once will give you good familiarity with the terms and concepts you will run into when you build your ad campaigns, but we see this chapter as more of a reference you will return to when you run into something you do not understand. As we have said before, the best way to learn Ads Manager is by using Ads Manager, but it is much easier when you have something to reference quickly when you are confused or in need of a quick definition.

Questions: Post Your Answers in our Free group at facebook.com/groups/fbinsta101

Do you feel like you have a clear understanding of the levels of an ad account? If you are still confused, post and let us know how we can help.

Did you find some of the features in the ad account structure that were interesting? If so, let us know which ones and why.

Are there any sections or settings that you don't understand at all? Post to let us know and we can help clear it up.

Key Takeaways:

Your ad account is made up of three levels, the campaign level, the ad set level, and the ad level

The Campaign level covers your ad campaign strategy, the ad set level covers targeting and placements, and the ad level covers building your ad and tracking elements

Getting comfortable with the conceptual structure and settings of the ad campaign will help you create better campaigns, faster.

Chapter 7 -

How do I know the right Zucking campaign strategy for my business?

Similar to the chapter on Facebook business pages, if I were to write a long, step-by-step chapter on how to develop an ad campaign strategy, it would not only be boring but it would be egregiously long. The reason it would be so long is that every choice within the ad campaign setup process spawns different choices as to what you need to do next. It is a lot like those old "choose your adventure books" where you had to read it and follow instructions to go to other sections of the book to see what happens based on your choices. I think they even did a Netflix show like that too. Anyway, as cool as that would be, it is close to impossible to do given the sheer volume of things you can do with Facebook ads. Having a lot of choices is not necessarily a bad thing. The fact that you can do a ton of specific things to advertise is why I think Facebook is the best ad platform for small businesses. It just limits the way people can write books about it.

Just to give you an idea of this complexity, in Ads Manager there are over 50 unique combinations of campaign objectives, conversion locations, and conversion goals to choose from when setting up your ad campaign. Each unique combo of those three settings creates a different way for you to get users on Facebook to interact with your business. If you think that sounds intimidating, I agree with you. For most small businesses though, their ad strategy follows the 80/20 rule. This is the rule where 80% of businesses are going to need only 20% or less of the unique options available to achieve their goals. The easiest way to reduce the scope of your campaign choices is to follow a series of simple questions that will guide you to the best ad campaign for your business.

The first question you want to ask is "What am I trying to achieve by running this ad campaign?" The choices are:

- Awareness - I want people to remember my ad

- Traffic - I want to send people to a destination
- Engagement - I want more messages, page likes, post engagement, or video views
- Leads - I want to collect information from people interested in my business
- App promotion - I want people to know I have an app and install it
- Sales - I want people to buy my products or services online

Now even though you may want to achieve some of these goals above there are certain requirements needed to run certain campaigns. For the most part, awareness, traffic, and engagement campaigns can be run without a complex setup. But, if you want to run a lead or sales campaign on your website, you will need to do advanced setup steps like adding conversion tracking, setting up lead capture questions and processes, making an online shop and catalog, or integrating your ad campaign with third-party software.

The most important part is that you know all of these exist so you can decide to run a less complicated campaign on your own or look to get more help and education if you want to run a more complex campaign.

The next question you want to ask is where do I want a customer to ultimately take a desired action? When you choose a campaign strategy, you are defining what you (the business) want to get from the campaign, but now you need to choose where you want that to occur. These are called conversion locations and their few options are shown below:

- Website or Landing Page
- Messaging apps - Messenger, WhatsApp, Instagram Direct
- Instagram Account
- Facebook Page

- Facebook Instant form
- Mobile App
- The ad itself
- Calls

The last question you would ask is how would I like Facebook to optimize my campaign. What would you like the algorithm to "get more of"? This performance goal varies based on the campaign objective you choose, but some of the more popular options are shown below:

- Maximize Reach of Ads - number of people who saw your ad at least once
- Maximize Daily Unique Reach - number of people who saw your ad at least once a day
- Maximize the number of Impressions - the number of times your ad was on screen
- Maximize ad recall lift - show ads to people most likely to remember them
- Maximize Video ThruPlays - People who watched at least 15 seconds of your video
- Maximize 2-second continuous views - People who watched at least 2 seconds of your video
- Maximize the number of Link Clicks - clicks on the ad that led to destinations on or off the platform
- Maximize the number of landing page views - the number of times a click resulted in the successful loading of a destination website, instant experience, or shop
- Maximize the number of calls - show your ad to people most likely to call your business
- Maximize the number of conversations - show your ad to people most likely to have a conversation through messaging

- Maximize the number of conversions - show your ad to people most likely to take action on your website
- Maximize the number of app events - show your ad to people most likely to take a pacific action on your app at least once
- Maximize the number of Page Likes - the number of times people like or follow your Facebook Business Page
- Maximize the number of leads - customer information you receive from connected business tools
- Maximize the number of app installs
- Maximize ROAS - Return on ad spend

Here is an example of how this could look when you are trying to figure out the best ad strategy:

What would most help your business?
- If people were aware you exist and know your brand?
- If people went to your website to learn about your products and services?
- If people engage with your ad or Facebook Page by liking, sharing, or commenting?
- If people filled out a lead form to contact you?
- If people knew about your app and downloaded it?
- If people bought your product online?
- If people send you a message directly?

It would help my business if people filled out a lead form to contact me!

Great, now where would you like people to fill out the contact form? We could:
- Send them to your website to fill out a form
- Fill out a form directly in the ad unit
- Collect lead information through messaging

Wow, I didn't know you could collect information right from the ad unit, let's do that!

OK, now we just need to know how to optimize the campaign. Would you like to:
- Maximize the total amount of leads you get from the ad unit
- Maximize the amount of conversion leads - which are leads Facebook believes will convert at a higher rate after sharing their info (PS - This will lower total lead count and cost more per lead).

I would like to get as many leads as possible, even if it means they are less likely to convert right away so I can add them to my database and market to them over time.

In this scenario we would create a campaign with the "Leads" Objective, selecting "Instant Forms" as the conversion location, and selecting "Maximize number of Leads" as the Performance goal.

Questions: Post Your Answers in our Free group at facebook.com/groups/fbinsta101
What combination of Objective / Conversion Location / Performance Goal do you think is right for your business?

Let us know if this was different than you expected. Were there options you didn't know existed?

How can you see this ad strategy delivering business outcomes to grow your company and why?

You can figure out your ad strategy by asking three simple questions:
> What do I want to get from my ad campaign?
> Where do I want this to take place?
> How do I want to optimize and improve?

If you choose a conversion location that leads somewhere off of Facebook, like a website or landing page, you will need to set up a Meta Pixel to track activity.

Choosing the right ad strategy for your business is one of the biggest factors in a successful campaign.

Chapter 8:
You'll Never Forget Your First…Ad Campaign

Ad Campaigns and Settings

As we venture into the hands-on experience of your first Facebook ad campaign, remember, that it's perfectly normal to feel a blend of excitement and nervous anticipation. It's kind of like when that beautiful dining room table you ordered online arrives in 4 boxes. You may be thinking, Did I get in over my head? How am I going to put this all together? Those are all perfectly valid thoughts, but you don't have to worry at all. It might seem complex at first glance, but with careful guidance and practice, you'll have a fully functioning ad campaign for your business. This chapter will bring all that you learned together so your experience is both smooth and successful. So, gather your notes, put on your marketing hat, and let's do this thing.

Open the ads manager and make sure you have the "campaigns" section selected, it should be the second icon down on the left-hand menu. In the upper left of the page you will see a large green button that says "+ create", click that button. The first thing you will see on your screen is a prompt to select your campaign objective. We covered campaign objectives in chapters 6 and 7, but to give you a quick refresher, this is where you answer the question, "What do I want from my ad campaign?" Select the campaign that best fits your strategy and click continue. After making that selection, the campaign is created and you are dropped directly into the campaign edit screen so you can adjust the remaining campaign settings before moving on to the next phase.

When you create the campaign, Facebook will automatically create a default Ad Set and Ad. You will see them in the menu structure on the left side of the campaign settings. This is a great illustration of the tiered campaign structure we talked about earlier in the book. The campaign level has a folder icon, which accurately represents the campaign as the highest level in the structure. The campaign level is where all of your ad sets and ads will be linked structurally. Underneath the campaign "folder" you will see the Ad set level which has four small squares next to the name. That icon represents the place where you can organize and share settings with multiple ads. Finally, you will see a singular square next to the Ad level. Here you can drill down on a particular ad within the ad set. You can quickly navigate to each level in the hierarchy by clicking on the level you wish to see, the menu will expand to show multiple ad sets and ads if you create more than one. By default, the name of your campaign will be "New (campaign objective) Campaign". You can keep that default name or change it in the "Campaign Name" section. After you are done there we can move on to the next section called "Special Ad Categories".

Special Ad Categories are a fairly new addition to Facebook's ad ecosystem. Over the years, certain advertising topics have been scrutinized by the US government as having the ability to be used in a way that is unethical or sometimes illegal. In response to this, Facebook created the Special Ad Category to limit the ad functionality of these topics so they can assure all advertisers comply with government regulations and reduce unethical behavior. There are four topics defined as special ad categories, they are: Credit, Employment, Housing, and Social Issues / Elections / Politics.

If your product or service falls into one of these categories you will still be able to run an ad campaign on Facebook, but you will notice that the audience targeting is extremely limited. Age, Gender, and detailed targeting will be pared down to a very small list or not available at all based on the type of special ad category chosen.

If you are thinking, what if I just don't choose anything and still run an ad for one of these topics? I would strongly suggest you don't. Facebook's ad review process is extremely sensitive and any attempt to purposely advertise against their terms of service can result in your ad being rejected or in some cases, your advertising privileges can be banned permanently.

False positives are also highly likely with anything that comes close to a Special Ad Category. The process is so sensitive that oftentimes ads that have nothing to do with the special ad categories still get rejected because they could be interpreted as being a flagged topic. For Example, "housing" is one of the special ad categories and covers buying, selling, or renting a home. Short-term rentals, like vacation homes, Airbnb, hotels, etc. are not included in the "housing" special ad category, but you may get an ad rejection notice anyway. If that does happen, Facebook offers an appeal process which in most cases resolves those issues.

Advantage Campaign Budget
Advantage Campaign Budget + is essentially letting Facebook take the wheel with how you spread the budget across your ad sets. This lets you set one central campaign budget and Facebook automatically allocates it across your ad sets & ads to get the best results based on your performance goals.

Setting a Budget That Works for You
The simplest first step is to decide how much money you can spend on your ads. It's a bit of a balancing act, you don't want to spend too much, but you also don't want to spend too little and miss out on reaching people. Your budget should match what you're trying to achieve with your business and feel right for what you can afford.

Your budget won't be the same as everyone else's because every business has different goals and situations. You have to think about what you need right now and what you're planning for in the future. Meta does not have a minimum spend level to get started, but we have seen that spending less than $25 a day may not deliver enough ads to allow Facebook to optimize the delivery of your ads and get enough results to make informed decisions after launching the campaign. If that sounds like too much, you can always start with a smaller amount and work your way up. The reason for the $ 25-a-day recommendation is to save time, but if you are not in a rush to expand and grow your business you can always start with a smaller amount. If you do not use a campaign budget, you can set a budget on the ad set level in the next chapter.

Did you run into any issues? If so, let us know what the issue was.

Do you think your business could fall into one of the special ad categories? If so, let us know which one, and we can help you navigate that.

Do you understand the concept of campaign Advantage+ budgeting? Campaign budgeting is a very useful and important tool in Facebook ads, if you need clarity on this, please post and let us know.

The most important part of the campaign settings is selecting a campaign objective, which we covered extensively in Chapter 7, be sure that the campaign objective you choose is right for your business.

Be sure to check if your campaign falls into one of the four special ad categories. If it does, you will need to take a less detailed approach to advertising.

Setting a budget is available at the campaign level, and if used will distribute the budget to your ad sets based on how Facebook deems most appropriate.

Chapter 9:
Ad Sets & Settings

If you remember when we first talked about ad sets in chapter 6, ad sets are groups or containers used for your ads so that they can share common settings. Ad sets are a fundamental component of Facebook advertising campaigns, acting as a bridge between your overarching campaign objectives and your ads. They allow you to define who you will target, how much you will spend, and where your ads will be placed. The way you structure your ad sets can significantly impact the success of your campaign. Proper organization ensures that each ad reaches the right audience, aligns with your budget constraints, and contributes to your overall campaign goals.

The conversion setting box will show right below your ad set name and contains the critical settings of conversion location and performance goal. These two settings define where you want your conversions to take place and how you want to define your ads' success. In the last chapter, we walked through campaign strategy, which included how to choose what your conversion location and goal should be. This is where you will assign those values to your ad set. You will also see an optional setting for cost per result goal, but as a beginning advertiser, you should avoid this setting as it can hurt your performance if you do not have the proper setup to use this feature.

The next section you will see under conversion settings is called Dynamic Creative. This is a setting that exists on the ad set level, but if you turn it on it will not affect the ad set themselves. What it will do is bring up expanded menu options within the ads contained in the ad set. We will expand on this more when we get to the next phase where we look at the ad settings and setup, but the short version is that dynamic creative allows you to use multiple images/videos, text, and headlines in one ad and Facebook will choose the combination of elements that they believe will be the most effective for your audience. In the next phase, we will go over the pros and cons of dynamic creative and how it can be used, but for now, I just want you to know what this setting is and where it is located.

After Dynamic Creative you will see the setting for Budget & Schedule. We will first go over the budgeting settings on the ad set level. If you recall from phase 1 there is a setting that allows you to set a budget for your whole campaign letting Facebook determine which ad sets and ads get the most budget based on what they determine to be most successful. If you have that selected in your campaign, you won't see the option to set budgets on the ad set level. But if you don't have that selected you will see the ability to control how much you want to spend on each ad set. You can set budgets either by defining a daily budget or a "lifetime" budget. If you set a daily budget, Facebook will serve your ad evenly throughout the day getting as close as possible to that exact amount every day. On the other hand, with a lifetime budget, you are telling Facebook the total amount you would like to spend on this ad set and you are not limiting the system to a particular daily spend. In this scenario, Facebook will serve your ad as it sees it will perform the best, so you may spend more on some days and less on others. In essence, you are just deciding on whether or not you want an even daily spend or not.

After making the decision on the daily or lifetime budget and entering an amount, you can set the total amount of time you want your ads to run by entering a start and end date. The start date is mandatory and the end date is optional. So if you wanted to spend $20 a day and run your ad set for 30 days, you can ensure it only spends a total of $600. Or, if you were using a lifetime budget, you could set that to $600 and run that ad set for 30 days. The only difference between these two examples is that in the daily budget scenario, you are telling Facebook to spend the budget evenly at $20 a day. In the lifetime budget scenario, you are allowing Facebook to spend more or less than $20 a day if it thinks it can get you better results, but in the end, will still spend a total of $600 over 30 days.

Audience Settings
Audience targeting is one of the most pivotal elements in understanding and effectively utilizing Facebook Ads. You don't want your audience to be just a group of random people who see your ad, you want them to be the right group of people. In this section, we will help you understand how to identify your target audience, how to leverage Facebook's targeting options, the importance of audience segmentation, and techniques for creating custom and lookalike audiences.

Knowing your target audience is one of the most important parts of successful advertising. Your audience should align with the people most likely to be interested in your product or service. This process involves analyzing your existing customer data to spot common characteristics and trends, such as age, gender, location, income level, and purchasing behaviors. Additionally, you should consider the behavioral aspects, which include interests, hobbies, values, and lifestyle choices. Surveys and feedback from current customers can provide invaluable insights into who your audience is. Most of the time a business owner, salesperson, support team lead, or anyone else who has daily conversations with customers can give valuable input needed to define a target audience. Once you have that information, Facebook has great audience targeting tools and settings to use for your ad campaign. They are:

Location Targeting: Allows you to reach customers in specific geographic locations, from entire countries to small towns, or even a radius around a location.

Demographic Targeting: This includes age, gender, education, occupation, and more

Interest Targeting: Facebook's algorithms allow you to target users based on their interests, activities, the pages they liked, and closely related topics. Facebook has an encyclopedic list of interests that is so big you can only really know what is included by searching.

Behavior Targeting: Target users based on purchase behaviors, device usage, and other activities.

Connection Targeting: Reach people who have a specific kind of connection to your page, app, or event.

Audience Segmentation
Audience segmentation is dividing your target audience into subgroups to tailor your messaging more precisely. This can significantly increase engagement and conversion rates. For example, you might create different ad sets for different age groups, geographic locations, or interests and then use images, videos, and copy that speak directly to them.

Crafting Custom and Lookalike Audiences
Custom Audiences are a powerful way to reconnect with people who have previously interacted with your business. You can create Custom Audiences from:

Customer Files: Use your existing customer data.

Website Traffic: Target people who have visited your website.

App Activity: Engage with those who have interacted with your app.

Offline Activity: Include interactions that happen offline, like in a store or over the phone.

Lookalike Audiences
Lookalike Audiences allow you to reach new people who are similar to your existing customers. To create a Lookalike Audience, you first need a source audience like a custom audience, people who have liked your page, or Instagram followers. Facebook will then use the source audience's likes and interests to create a list of new people similar to them that you can use in your ad set's targeting.

Best Practices for Audience Settings
Start Broad, Then Refine: Begin with a wider audience and gradually narrow down based on performance data.

Test and Learn: Test different audiences in different ad sets to see which ones respond best.

Keep It Fresh: Regularly update your Custom Audiences to ensure relevancy.

Balance Size and Relevance: Larger audiences offer scale, but smaller audiences can offer higher relevance and engagement.

Mastering audience settings in your ad sets is a journey of understanding your customers and using that knowledge to create more targeted, effective advertising. Remember, the better you know your audience, the more successful your Facebook ads will be. Keep experimenting, refining, and learning to unlock the full potential of your Facebook advertising campaign.

Lynnesight - Advantage+ options, as we mentioned earlier, is Facebook's suite of products that use AI to help find the best audience and placements. You can use Advantage+ targeting instead of creating ad sets based on handpicked interests, locations, demographics, and custom audiences. When you use Advantage+, Facebook will use their first-party AI and data they have using your business page, ad history, website, and ads similar to yours and create an audience to target your ideal customer. You can also select Advantage+ targeting and add a few audience suggestions to help the AI learn faster and hopefully bring better results. Facebook seems to be pushing using their Advantage products more and more over time. In fact, for most new ad sets you will see Advantage+ as the main option for audience targeting, with a small link underneath to "switch" to manual targeting as a secondary option. We have seen using Advantage+ and handpicked audience settings be successful for our clients. It all comes down to testing. There is no one right way to do anything on Facebook, and this is a perfect example. It is a good option to have if you do not want to go through the trouble of selecting a bunch of audience targeting options, but also run the risk of going too broad and lowering your performance. There is no way to know until you try. AI technology is moving so fast that by the time you read this, it could be completely different.

Ad Placement settings
The last setting in the ad set level is called "Placements". Ad placement refers to where your ads can appear across all four Meta platforms which include Facebook, Instagram, Audience Network, and Messenger. Each placement option offers unique advantages so it is important to understand how each one works so you can choose the ones that apply to your campaign goals and target audience.

Ad Placement Options:

1. Feeds

The feed is the heart of the experience and one of the most popular placement options. This is what most Facebook & Instagram users see every day while scrolling through posts from friends and influencers they follow. The feed offers:

High Visibility: Your ads appear directly in the user's central content feed.

Engagement Opportunities: This placement typically yields high engagement rates due to its prominent position amongst user-generated posts.

Versatility: Great for various ad formats, including images, videos, and carousels.

2. Stories & Reels

Stories are user-generated full-screen, vertical videos and images that appear for 24 hours, offering an immersive experience. The limited time that user-generated Stories appear helps to incent users to check them often, which gives your ads a high likelihood of being seen. Some of the unique features of Stories include:

Interactive Features: Advertisers can use interactive elements like polls and swipe-up links to engage viewers.

Spontaneous and Timely: Ideal for timely promotions or spontaneous content, mirroring the fleeting nature of Stories.

Reach and Engagement: They offer a wide reach, appearing at the top of the app, and often have higher engagement due to their prominent placement and format.

Reels are short, engaging videos that offer a creative and entertaining way to showcase products or services. They are vertical videos recommended less than 60 seconds (30 being preferred). Short-form video is extremely popular due to the rise of short-form video platforms like TikTok and Instagram, some of the unique advantages include:

> Discoverability: High potential for virality and discoverability, especially through the Explore page.

> Creative Freedom: Advertisers can experiment with trends, music, and creative editing to capture attention.

> Integration with Shopping: Reels can be integrated with Instagram & Facebook Shops, allowing for direct product tagging and purchases.

Both Stories and Reels provide an authentic way for brands to connect with their audience, leveraging the casual and creative nature of these formats. They are particularly effective for reaching younger demographics who prefer dynamic and interactive content. The formats also allow for detailed performance tracking, enabling advertisers to analyze the impact of their campaigns.

3. In-Stream Ads for Videos and Reels

If you plan on using video content, you can advertise before, during, or after they watch a video or reel using in-stream ad placements. Both In-Stream Ads for Videos and Ads in Reels represent a shift towards more integrated and less intrusive advertising, aligning with user preferences for seamless content experiences. They offer advertisers a way to reach audiences during their engagement with entertaining or informative video content, potentially leading to higher engagement and conversion rates compared to traditional ad formats.

4. Search Results

Both Facebook and Instagram's search result ad placements offer advertisers a way to connect with users at a moment of active interest or intent, which can be particularly effective for driving awareness, consideration, or conversions. As users are already in a mode of discovery or seeking information, well-placed and relevant ads in search results can be a powerful tool for reaching potential customers.

5. Messages

Facebook and Instagram have expanded their advertising offerings to include placements within their messaging platforms, providing a unique avenue for businesses to reach their audience. These placements include inbox ads that appear in the main chat list of the Messenger app, blending in with the user's conversations. They are labeled as "Sponsored" to distinguish them from regular messages. The other message placement is called sponsored messages. Here businesses can send personalized messages directly to users who have previously interacted with their Messenger account. This allows for targeted promotions or updates.

6. Apps and sites

The "Apps & Sites" ad placement in Facebook refers to the ability of advertisers to place ads across a network of third-party mobile apps and websites, which is facilitated through the Facebook Audience Network. Ads can appear in various formats, including native, banner, interstitial, and in-stream video ads, allowing advertisers to choose the best format for their message and target audience. Some of the unique benefits include:

Increased Reach and Frequency: Expanding ad placement to third-party apps and websites allows businesses to reach their audience more frequently and in different contexts.

Cost-Effective: It can be a cost-effective way to reach more people, as the Audience Network often has lower costs per impression or click compared to ads placed directly on Facebook.

Consistent Experience: Ads maintain a consistent quality and relevance of Facebook's native advertising, providing a seamless experience for users.

Performance Tracking: Advertisers can track the performance of their ads across the network, just as they would for ads placed directly on Facebook, using the same metrics and tools.

Lynnesight: As I've mentioned before, Meta has an option called Advantage+ that you can utilize in a few areas. Here in Ad placements, there is an option to select "Advantage+ Placements" which will use AI to serve your ads in the placements they think will perform best. Unless you click "Manual Placements" you won't even see the other placement options we just mentioned. The "Advantage+ Placements" option is a great tool and we use it often for ourselves and our clients, especially if you don't want to stress over the details of each placement and whether you should use it or not. There is a way to see what the Meta recommended placements are by clicking on "Manual placements" and seeing which ones are automatically selected, which are typically the ones that Advantage+ recommends. You can choose to keep them or add/delete any of the options as well. We typically let the

AI do its job unless there is a specific reason for going in and changing it. For example, if I check the Advanced Ad Preview and see that our creative does not fit or will not serve in certain placements, I will go back and uncheck that placement using the manual option. You can also use the manual placement option if you want to test placements against each other like Facebook feed ads vs Instagram feed ads. In this method, you would use identical ad sets with the only difference being the ad placement.

Questions: Post Your Answers in our Free group at facebook.com/groups/fbinsta101

Did you run into any issues? If so, what was the issue and how can we help?

If you used detailed targeting, let us know what demographics, interests, or behaviors surprised you when they showed up. Why was it surprising?

Did you choose manual placements or did you leave that to Advantage+ Placements? If you chose manual placements, let us know why you chose those specific placements.

<u>**Key Takeaways:**</u>

The Ad set level had some of the most important settings in your ad account including Conversion location, Performance Goal, and Detailed Targeting.

If you choose a conversion location and/or performance goal that leads to a website or landing page, you will need to set up the Meta Pixel or CAPI to track performance.

You can choose to input your detailed targeting like demographics & interests, or use Advantage+ targeting if you want Facebook to choose what they think is best. This is still in early development, but some advertisers have found great success with Advantage+. You have to test and learn to know what is best for your campaign.

Although you have the option to select individual placements, we would recommend letting Facebook's Advantage+ Placements optimize your placements when you are first getting started.

Chapter 10:
Creating an Ad

Finally, you have arrived at the last step before officially launching your ad campaign. Thankfully, we have covered a lot of what you will need to know to create an ad so we will focus on the process and sections in the ad platform.

You should see that a generic ad has already been created for each ad set in your campaign. The ad should be titled "New (whatever campaign objective you choose) Ad". The first section you will see is Ad Name. While nothing is forcing you to change the name of the ad, we highly recommend that you do. When you start running your campaign and looking at dashboards and performance you will not have the luxury of seeing the ad set and campaign like you do when you first set it up, which is why it is important to name the ad in a way that identifies it properly. For Example, if you have an ad in a traffic campaign, targeting a specific location, using a picture of a white house, you can name it "Traffic Texas House Ad". This way when you look at it in a list of your other ads, you understand the context when viewing its performance. Imagine looking at a list of ads that just say New Traffic Ad 1, 2, 3, 4…that doesn't help much when you are trying to understand what works or not.

You can skip the partnership ad section, as that pertains to more advanced co-branding situations, and move to the Identity Section. Here you need to choose the Facebook Business Page you are using and, if you have an Instagram account, you can connect that here as well.

Now on to the Ad creation process. You will see a dropdown that has "Create Ad" selected, if you click on the dropdown you can see options for "Use Existing Post" or "Use Creative Hub mockup", we are going to focus on creating an ad manually so leave "Create ad" selected.

Next, you will need to choose your creative source. For 99% of ads, you will be using Manual upload to get your desired image or video into Facebook's Ad system, but if you have already created a catalog for a shop or online store, you can select from that catalog here. You will also have to choose the format of your ad. Here you will see choices for a single image or video, carousel, or collection. We described these in detail back in Chapter 6, so just choose the one you would like. Most often you will be using the Single Image or Video option, so that is what we will focus on in this example. You may see an option for "Multi-advertiser ads" which is recommended by Facebook. Multi-advertiser ads can help people discover and compare products and services from multiple businesses. This ad unit, available for select placements on Facebook and Instagram, allows you to be discovered by people who have recently shown an interest in products or businesses. Unless you have a particular issue with having your ad shown alongside other businesses like yours, you can keep this option checked.

In the Ad Creative section, you will begin to build your ad combining media, ad copy, headlines, and a call to action. We went over each of these in Chapter 6, so hopefully you have an idea of what to use for these sections. First, add your media (video or image) by selecting it from the media drop-down. When you click on the selection, a pop-up will appear allowing you to upload your media using the "+ Upload" button. When the upload is complete, select it and click next. You may see images and videos that you have uploaded for use on your Facebook Business page or past campaigns, which you are free to use in your ad. The next step shows how your media will appear in different formats, allowing you to "crop" images to fit or upload new images that are created in the correct ratio for that placement. After the cropping stage, click next to get to the optimization phase. Here, you can see your media in all formats with Facebook's suggestions to optimize the use of media in that placement. Unless you have a particular reason not to, it is recommended to follow the optimizations given as that will help Facebook be able to serve your ad properly. Click done to apply the optimizations and get back to the ad creative setup screen.

Lynnesight: There are many times in the "crop" section that I ignore the 'suggested' ratio option. Often 'original' is the best way to show your image or video as sometimes the suggestions will crop it too much or show it oddly. You can toggle back and forth between the two options to see which is best for your particular creative. Also, make sure that your image is centered. Sometimes when you use their suggestion it has the image offset but you can slide it over to make it correct.

You will now see your image or video in the "ad preview" section directly to the right. The Ad Preview tool is a great way to see how the elements you add to your ad (LOL) show up to users in certain placements. The preview section defaults to the "Feeds" placement, but you can see how it looks for all placements if you click the "Advanced Preview" button to the right.

Ad Copy
Now that you have added your image or video, we can move on to the text, headline, and call to action. The first section, called primary text, is the long-form ad copy that I am sure you have seen when scrolling past ads in your feed. In a Facebook ad, the primary text is displayed above the image or video. It's the first piece of text a viewer reads, making it essential for capturing attention. It usually contains the core message of the ad, highlighting the benefits, features, or any promotional offers. While there's no strict limit on length, shorter texts are often more effective. Facebook recommends keeping the primary text under 125 characters to ensure readability and engagement. If your text

is longer than the viewable space on your ad, users can click "see more" to expand and read the entire text. You can use the ad preview section to see exactly where and how much of your text is being shown before being cut off by "see more". While it is not 100% perfect, it is a good guide to use so you make sure the most important parts of your text are viewable without a click.

On Instagram, the primary text appears below the image or video, unlike Facebook. This placement aligns with how users typically engage with Instagram posts. Given Instagram's visual-centric nature, the primary text should complement the imagery, adding context or additional information to the visual content. You can use the Advanced Preview button to see how your text looks in all ad formats.

In both platforms, the primary text is an opportunity to directly communicate with the audience, contextualize the visual content, and persuade users to take action. It's a space where advertisers craft their message to resonate with their target audience, reflecting the campaign's goals and the brand's personality. Effective primary text is clear, engaging, and aligned with the overall objective of the ad.

Headline
The ad headline in Facebook and Instagram ads is a critical component that captures attention and conveys the core message or offer of the advertisement. On Facebook, the headline is prominently displayed below the image or video component of the ad and is designed to quickly grab the viewer's attention, summarize the ad's value proposition, and call the user to action. The headline is a key component of whether a user stops to engage with the rest of the ad content. Like the primary text, there's no strict character limit, but shorter headlines (usually under 40 characters) are recommended for clarity and impact.

Longer headlines may be truncated, especially on mobile devices. This is another great way to use the ad preview to see if your headline is fully visible to users. Effective Facebook ad headlines are usually concise, clear, and directly related to the product or service being advertised. They often include a key benefit or a compelling offer.

On Instagram, the ad headline appears in a similar position as on Facebook, below the visual content. However, due to the platform's layout, it might be less immediately noticeable than the primary text. This is why it is important to have a strong first few sentences of primary text because that is what is mostly shown on Instagram ad placements.

The headline is a powerful tool to capture interest, deliver a clear message, and encourage further engagement, whether it's reading more, clicking on a link, or exploring a product. A well-crafted headline can significantly enhance the overall impact and success of the ad.

CTA (Call to Action)
The Call-to-Action (CTA) in Facebook and Instagram ads is a critical component that guides users toward a specific action or response, directly influencing the effectiveness of the advertisement. On Facebook, the CTA is typically presented as a clickable button located below the ad copy and headline. Advertisers can choose from a variety of CTA options from the dropdown menu, such as "Shop Now," "Learn More," "Sign Up," "Book Now," or "Contact Us." Depending on the objective and offer of your ad, you can choose the one that matches best. Clicking the CTA button typically takes the user to a landing page, product page, form, or another destination set by the advertiser, aligned with the ad's goal.

In both Facebook and Instagram ads, the CTA is essential for driving user engagement and achieving the ad's objectives. It serves as a clear directive to the audience, encouraging them to take the next step, whether it's making a purchase, learning more about a product or service, or connecting with a brand. Much like the headline, the effectiveness of a CTA can significantly influence the conversion rate and overall success of an ad campaign.

The only section left in the Ad phase is tracking. We will cover tracking in detail in the next chapter. If you are using a campaign objective with a conversion location that is "on-platform" it means it doesn't leave the Meta family of apps like Messenger, WhatsApp, Instagram Direct, Instagram Accounts, Facebook Pages, Facebook Instant form, etc. You do not have to worry about tracking because if you stay within Meta-owned properties, they can track all advertising activity.

If you are using or plan to use a conversion location "off-platform" AKA a website or web surface not owned by Meta, you will need to understand and use tracking tools and techniques for Meta to gather information on your ad campaigns. If you are using off-platform conversions, you will need to pay close attention to the information in the next chapter as you will not be able to set up most of these campaigns without proper tracking.

If everything is ready to go, and you do not need advanced tracking, you can click Review & Publish at the top of the screen and you will be off and running!

Did you run into any issues? If so, let us know what the issue was.

What ad type did you choose to start with? Did you do multiple versions including video? If you still need help with ad creative, please post and we will do our best to answer your questions.

<u>**Key Takeaways:**</u>

Your ad is your connection with the customer, make sure you do your best to use images, video, copy, and headlines that speak to your ideal customer and get their attention

It is good to start with at least two versions of an ad, three is even better. The more versions you test, the better chance of finding one that performs well.

Don't just use different images and videos to test multiple ads, test different headlines, ad copy, and CTA's as well.

Chapter 11: Understanding Meta Ad Tracking

To track advertising that occurs on "off-platform" websites, Facebook and Instagram use ad-tracking tools that enable businesses to measure, optimize, and build audiences for their advertising campaigns. These tools include the Facebook Pixel, Events, and Conversions API. If you are familiar with web technology these terms may sound familiar, but for the rest of you, these may sound like tools better used to fix a spaceship than track digital advertising. This is perfectly fine as we will explain what these tools are and how they work. If you want to go into how to install these for use on your website, I would suggest you "do not try this at home" and instead work with a web professional to ensure it is done properly.

Facebook Pixel & Events
The Facebook Pixel is the most common tracking tool of the Facebook and Instagram advertising ecosystem. It's not a tiny dot on your screen or a digital fairy that grants wishes. It is a small yet powerful piece of code that is embedded into your website. The pixel's job is to collect valuable data about how users interact with your site and report that information back to your advertising campaigns. Much like the nosey neighbor on your street, the Facebook pixel knows who visited your site after clicking your ad, what they looked at, or if they bought something vs just a window shop. This interaction data is critical in understanding and analyzing user behavior in response to your ads.

Beyond mere tracking, one of the greatest features of the Facebook Pixel lies in its ability to enhance targeting and remarketing strategies. When people visit your website and do stuff like look at products or put things in their cart, the Pixel keeps track of all that. Then, when you want to show ads to people on Facebook & Instagram, you can use this information to make your ads super relevant to what they like or are interested in. This is great because it means your ads will pop up for people who are more likely to be interested in what you're selling. For example, if someone was looking at a pair of shoes on your website but didn't buy them, the Pixel remembers and helps you show those shoes again in your ads to that same person. This little reminder can sometimes be just the thing they need to go back and buy those shoes. When you are scrolling on Facebook and Instagram and see an ad for a product or service you found on your laptop earlier in the day, that's not magic, it's the Facebook pixel.

In short, the Facebook Pixel is important because it not only keeps an eye on what people do on your site but also helps you make your ads a lot more personal and effective. This means you're more likely to get people interested in what you're selling, and they're more likely to buy it.

"Events" take the usage of the Facebook Pixel to the next level. Events are digital markers that are designed to track specific actions or "events" that users can perform on your website. You can think of events like booby traps hidden inside the functionality of your site. For example, if you want to set an "event" on a certain button on your homepage, the pixel knows to track that button click by placing the event code on it. When someone clicks that button, the "booby trap" is set off and the pixel counts that action. I feel like I just set a record for the most uses of "booby trap" in a book about social media advertising.

Events are separated into two major categories. First, there are "standard events." Facebook has already set these up with pre-written code that is instantly recognized in any Meta ad campaign. These include actions like 'Add to Cart', indicating a user showing interest in a product, or 'Purchase', signaling the completion of a sale. Each of these actions tells you a bit about what your customers like and do on your site. Facebook has 15 standard events, but the most prominent are:

ViewContent: When a visitor views a page or content on your site, such as a product page.

AddToCart: When a product is added to the shopping cart on your site.

InitiateCheckout: When a user begins the checkout process.

Purchase: When a purchase is completed.

Lead: When a user expresses interest in your offering, such as by signing up for a trial or filling out a form.

CompleteRegistration: When a user completes a registration form, such as for a subscription service.

Subscribe: When a user subscribes to a service or a newsletter.

Then, there are "custom events." These custom events are special because you create them based on what's important for your business. For instance, your business may have different levels of service that people can choose from. Using a standard event you would only be able to track if someone signed up for a service, but will not differentiate which one. Using custom events you can track if ads are selling higher-cost services vs lower-cost services which is important to know if you are trying to get more revenue for your investment. Custom events let you focus on the things that matter to your business. So if you want to get more specific in your tracking, talk to a developer about helping you with custom event tracking.

Now, why are the Facebook Pixel and Events so crucial? By understanding which actions are most frequently completed and by whom, Facebook's advertising algorithm can more accurately target audiences who are likely to take similar actions. This kind of targeting is not just throwing darts in the dark; it's more like using a laser-guided system to reach the exact audience segment that would find your ads most relevant.

Additionally, events are integral to reporting and analytics. This data isn't just a bunch of numbers and charts; it's a goldmine of insights, telling you what's working and what's not. By analyzing event data, you can measure the direct impact of your ads, understand customer behaviors, and ultimately make data-driven decisions to refine your campaigns.

How Apple's IOS 14 Update Changed Meta Ad Tracking
When Apple updated its iPhone software (iOS) to iOS 14 on September 16, 2020, it changed how ads can track people's actions. iOS is the system that makes iPhones and other Apple devices like iPads and iPhones work. With this new update, Apple introduced something called the App Tracking Transparency (ATT) framework. Now, whenever you download an app on your Apple device, the app has to ask if it's okay to track what you do on other apps and websites. Before this update, apps could track a lot of this stuff without asking.

This was a big deal for advertisers, especially those who use Facebook and Instagram to show their ads. Now, a lot more people choose not to be tracked because they get to decide. This means advertisers get less information about what people do online, making it harder to create targeted and personal ads.

Facebook, which Meta owns, had to quickly adjust to these changes. They came up with a new way to track things, called Aggregated Event Measurement. This new system fits with

Apple's privacy rules but still lets advertisers track some user actions, though not as many as before.

Also, Facebook had to limit how many different types of actions (like making a purchase or signing up for something) they could track. Advertisers now have to be more selective about what actions are most important to track for their business.

Overall, Apple's iOS 14 update made privacy a lot more important in digital advertising. It forced advertisers and platforms like Facebook to find new ways to track ads while respecting people's privacy choices. This shift meant they had to balance being effective in advertising with following these new privacy rules.

Other important tracking considerations

Understanding how to track where sales come from (called "attribution models") has become more complicated with the new privacy rules in Apple's iOS 14 update. Before, advertisers could easily see how their ads led to sales or sign-ups over a certain period. But now, with more privacy-focused rules, this time frame (or "attribution window") is shorter and not as clear. This makes it harder for advertisers to figure out exactly how much their ads are helping. So, advertisers need to really understand these new rules and maybe even change how they measure their ad success to make sure they're getting it right.

Another big thing nowadays is the importance of first-party data. This is information you collect directly from your customers, like what they do on your website, what they buy, or if they sign up for something. Since it's getting harder to use data from other sources (third-party data), the info you collect yourself is super valuable. It's also better for privacy because you get it straight from your customers with their permission. Advertisers are now focusing a lot on getting this kind of data. They're trying to talk more directly with customers, find better ways to collect their data and use this info to make ads that speak to people's interests.

In short, these days advertisers have to think a lot about privacy, really understand how to track ad success, especially after the iOS 14 changes, and put more effort into getting and using their customer data. Successfully advertising online now means knowing the legal stuff, being able to change your strategies, and building good, honest relationships with your customers.

Conversions API (CAPI)

Facebook's Conversions API (CAPI) is a special tool that helps advertisers deal with the new privacy rules from Apple's iOS 14 update. These rules made it harder to track what people do on apps and websites.

CAPI works differently from older ways of tracking, like the Facebook Pixel. Instead of relying on tracking data from your browser, it sends data straight from your website's server to Facebook. This is handy because even if someone using an iPhone says they don't want to be tracked, you can still understand how they interact with your ads, but in a privacy-friendly way.

Since Apple's update makes it hard for browsers and apps to track user activities, CAPI acts like a detour. It keeps track of important actions like when someone buys something or signs up on your website. This way, it's not as affected by the new tracking limits from iOS 14.

With CAPI, you can still figure out how well your ads are working and plan your ad campaigns better. Even though tracking on iPhones has been cut down, CAPI gives you important info to help make your ads better.

CAPI also fits well with the new privacy rules. It only sends the data that's needed, and it does this in a way that keeps user information private. This means you can track your ads without breaking any privacy laws.

Overall, CAPI is a good way to keep tracking ads and understanding how they perform, even with the new privacy changes from Apple. However, setting it up can be tricky. It's more complicated than just using the Facebook Pixel. But, the good news is that many website platforms like WordPress, Shopify, Wix, and HubSpot are making it easier. They're creating simple ways to set up CAPI without needing to be a tech expert.

Lynnesight: As Rob mentioned at the end of the previous chapter, if you are not planning on doing ads off the platform AKA to a website, you do not need to worry about this part. If this sounds too overwhelming or like another language, don't let this stop you from trying to run ads. If you aren't the most tech-savvy or do not have access to someone who can help with pixels, CAPI, and events, I highly recommend starting with running 'on platform ads' like click-to-message, instant forms, or simply a likes campaign. Using these campaigns, you can start practicing using Ad sets, building ads, and looking at metrics without worrying about tracking anything to a website. You can learn a lot about your ideal audience, ad copy, and ad creativity by just doing ads on the platform. Many businesses don't even have or like their website, so they never use it. Meta has created many options (and sometimes prefers) for you to do everything right on Facebook and Instagram. So do not let all of this tracking talk deter you from running ads, just cut out the website altogether!

How advanced is the tracking that you need? Is it just the pixel, pixel plus events, or CAPI? If you are still confused about tracking, please post and let us know.

Do you think you need to get assistance with installing tracking? If you think you need help with tracking, and don't know what to do, please post and let us know.

<u>**Key Takeaways:**</u>

If you are not digitally savvy, do not attempt to implement these tracking tools yourself. Get help from someone who has experience with this.

Using events takes your tracking and optimization to a new level allowing you to see each step in the conversion process.

CAPI is the best method to track ad performance but is also the most difficult to implement. Be sure to check if one of the web platforms you use has a CAPI integration which can make installation simple.

Chapter 12:

Is this the end, or just the beginning?

Now that you have gone through the process of learning, strategizing, and launching your ads, we enter into the crucial journey that begins after you've launched the ad campaign. While setting up and launching your campaign might feel like a significant achievement, it's important to understand that the launch of your ad campaign is the starting point of a more intricate process. The real digital advertising work happens in the post-launch stages where monitoring, adjusting, and learning from your campaign become the keys to success.

Once your campaign is live, your ads become part of a dynamic and interactive playground. Here, your ads interact with real users, compete for attention among other content, and generate valuable data you can use for evaluation and optimization. This stage is crucial because it provides real-world feedback on your advertising strategies, revealing how well your ads resonate with your target audience.

The process of monitoring your campaign involves keeping a watchful eye on various performance metrics. This data isn't just a collection of numbers; it's direct feedback about how users are receiving and interacting with your ads. Are they clicking through? Are they engaging with the content? Are they taking the actions you intended? These are the questions that your monitoring efforts will help answer.

Watching and gathering data is only part of the process. The real skill lies in interpreting this information and using it to make informed adjustments to your campaign. This approach is what sets successful digital advertisers apart. It involves fine-tuning your ads based on performance metrics, experimenting with different creatives, tweaking your target audience, and reassessing your budgets. The digital advertising space is fast-paced and ever-changing, requiring you to be agile and responsive.

Facebook & Instagram ads in particular can change quickly because of how fast things move on the platform. What's popular on Facebook changes often, and this can affect how well your ads do. For example, an ad might be doing great one week, but then not so well the next week because of these changes. This means you have to keep a close eye on your ads and be ready to change your plans quickly to keep up with how fast Facebook changes. It's important to be flexible and adjust your ads often to get the best results.

Finally, you'll learn the importance of learning from your campaign performance. Every ad campaign, whether successful or not, is a treasure trove of insights. Understanding what worked and what didn't is invaluable for refining your future strategies. It's about building upon each experience to enhance your skills and approach to digital advertising.

Setting Expectations
Getting quick success with digital ads, especially on social platforms like Facebook and Instagram, isn't common. It's different from traditional ads where you might predict results more easily. In digital ads, there are many things to consider like how people behave online, how the platforms sort things, the quality of your ads, and changing trends on social media. Even a good plan might not work fast.

There are only a handful of times in my career where I launched an ad campaign and got immediate success, exactly how I planned it, with no adjustments needed. Those are the exception, not the rule. If you're new to this, I want you to let that sink in. If you ask anyone in the industry they will tell you the same thing.

This common misconception discourages new advertisers who may have learned to do ads themselves using generic training that does not tell you what to expect AFTER you launch the campaign. The best advice is to be patient and focus on long-term goals. Successful online advertisers try out dozens of different types of ads, targeting groups, and creative ideas before finding what works best. Learning from prior performance using trial and error is a big part of being successful with Facebook and Instagram ads.

The time it takes to see true business success results from your ads can vary a lot from campaign to campaign. It depends on what you're selling, how well your ads initially resonate with your target audience, and how well you've researched your market. Even then, you could have done all the research in the world and it still doesn't work. Don't let that discourage you and quit. The best advertisers out there aren't better than you, they just stuck it out until they figured out what works. Sometimes, it might take weeks or months to understand if your ads are or aren't working, only to find out they aren't and you need to adjust.

Another factor leading to variable performance is that digital advertising is always changing. What works now might not work later. So, being flexible, always learning, and ready to change your strategies is very important. Being patient, persistent, and open to learning from both wins and losses will serve you well as you get more experience with ads. Even the experts will tell you that what they were doing a year ago, is not what they are doing today, and will likely not be what they are going to be doing in six months. The important part is to get in the game, learn, and adjust your way to success.

Questions: Post Your Answers in our Free group at
facebook.com/groups/fbinsta101

What, if anything, stood out when you observed your ad metrics
after you first launched the campaign?

Are you seeing anything that you can deem an immediate
success? Let us know so we can celebrate your win.

Have you looked at other ads on Facebook differently now that
you know how they work? Let us know if your perspective has
changed.

<u>**Key Takeaways:**</u>

Look at your campaign often in the first few weeks after it launches, be sure to note anything out of the ordinary, good or bad.

Very few campaigns are immediately successful. Allow your campaign time to gather data before making any changes or optimizations.

Do some research. Look at other ads on Facebook and do some Google searches on the latest trends and news.

Want to know how to see anyone's ads on Facebook?

Follow These Steps:

1. Go to a business's Facebook Page
2. Click the "About" section
3. Select "Page Transparency"
4. See if the page is "Currently Running Ads" or Not
5. If they are, click "See All"
6. Scroll to the bottom and click on "Go to Ad Library"
7. Look at all the ads!

PS - if you go to www.facebook.com/ads/library you can search ads by country, category, or keyword.

Chapter 13:
Understanding Analytics

First things first, what is analytics? Analytics refers to the collection, analysis, and interpretation of data for your ad campaigns. These platforms provide a wealth of data points such as reach (how many people see your ad), engagement (how people interact with your ad), click-through rates (how often people click on your ad), and conversion rates (how often clicks turn into desired actions like sales or sign-ups). By analyzing these metrics, you gain invaluable insights into your audience's behaviors and preferences, the effectiveness of your ad content, and the overall return on your advertising investment. Essentially, analytics is the process of using digital metrics & measurements to analyze your ads performance (Analyze + Metrics = Analytics).

Navigating Facebook and Instagram Analytics

The most important thing to remember when you are first diving into the metrics of your ads is to try not to get overwhelmed. There are hundreds of metrics available to you in the ads manager, but much like the settings for your campaign, not all of them will be relevant to the way you are running ads or the goals you are trying to achieve.

After your campaign goes live, you can go to the campaign overview screen by clicking the campaign icon in the left menu of the ads manager. It should be the second icon down on the list. Like in the campaign setup, you will see tabs on the top of the page letting you quickly see these metrics on the campaign, ad set, and ad level. Another important thing to remember is that it is really easy to switch from tab to tab which may show you different numbers and columns. So make sure you are always aware of what tab is selected when looking at your metrics.

Below the Ads tab on the top right, you will see an icon that looks like three vertical bars. That "columns" selector allows you to pick a preset selection of metrics that align with the ad strategy you may be using. There are presets for performance, performance and clicks, engagement, delivery, and video engagement. If you hover over each selection you can see all the metrics available in each preset. The performance and clicks preset have the best starting set of metrics, so I suggest you start there. You can also customize your columns at the bottom of the preset selector menu if you want to add or remove columns from your view. Once you change the columns from the preset, you will be using a custom view.

Now that you have performance and clicks preset selected for columns and you are on the campaign tab, you should see your campaign name followed by the 21 columns of metrics in that preset. That may sound overwhelming, but you won't be using many of them once you get a feel for how to read your campaign data. Scrolling through the columns you can see that some metrics are self-explanatory, and some may sound like a foreign language. Don't worry, I speak analytics and can translate. Working from left to right, I'll outline the ones written in "advertisers" below.

Lynnesight: Try not to get overwhelmed here! This would be a perfect time to jump into the Facebook group and ask questions! While the preset 'performance and clicks' is a great place to start, there may be other metrics that you should also be looking at depending on your specific campaign and performance goal. We can help guide you to see if you should add any additional metrics columns to the reporting and help you interpret idea ranges for metrics, etc.

Delivery - This shows you the current status of your campaign, ad set, or ads depending on what tab you have selected. If they are running normally, the status will be "active". Campaigns, ad sets, and ads can have different delivery statuses, so be sure to check each tab to make sure you don't miss anything. Delivery can also show you if the campaign is off, in the draft if you are editing, in the process if it is in the process of being approved, rejected, or error if there is an issue or learning.

I will take a second to explain the learning status. As we said earlier, Facebook will try its best to deliver the performance goal you chose as the primary metric for success. When a campaign first launches, Facebook uses all the settings you gave in the setup phase and begins serving your ads trying to figure out what will work best on the platform to get your primary metric. While this is going on, the delivery will show the status of "learning". You should try your best not to change anything in the campaign while it is in the learning phase as you can delay the process and hurt performance. There is no set time for a campaign to stay in the learning phase, but since it is based on the algorithm figuring out what is best by testing your ad across various placements and targets, giving it more budget to "learn" in the beginning could help speed up the process. Not all campaigns will have a learning phase, so don't freak out if the campaign goes right to an active state.

Results - Everyone knows what results are, but what results? Isn't everything technically a result? What Facebook is saying is "performance goal results". Based on what performance goal you chose, that metric will show in the "Results" column. Some common results could be landing page views, clicks, conversations, and leads.

Reach - in digital advertising, reach refers to how many unique people see your ad. If you see 100 in the reach column, it means your ads were served to 100 different people.

Impressions - this refers to the total number of times your ad is shown on users' screens. This metric counts every instance in which your ad appears to users, regardless of whether the same person sees the ad multiple times or if it's seen by different people.

It is important to note that just because your ad is shown on a user's screen, it doesn't mean they see it. Facebook tracking is good, but it's not that good. Depending on the placement, there are higher probabilities people will see an ad impression or not, but there is no way to see how many ad impressions were seen. If you are new and haven't read an amazing book written by amazing people you may be misled on the importance of Impressions. We have had several clients who ran ads with other media providers before working with us say, "Hey, my ad was doing great with X agency, they got me 100,000 impressions a month". After I explained how impressions work, they were less excited. Impressions are an important metric, but not by itself. When we get to some of the more important calculated metrics, you will see how impressions help develop rates and percentages that are vital to measuring performance.

Frequency - is a metric that represents the average number of times an individual has had your ad appear on their page. It is a calculated metric found by dividing the total number of impressions (the total times your ad was displayed) by the reach (the total number of unique individuals who saw your ad). Frequency is an important metric because you may want people to see your ad multiple times, but also may want to avoid them seeing it too much. Frequency allows you to keep your ad in the space between.

CPM - CPM is a pricing model used to denote the cost of an advertisement per 1,000 impressions. This means when you choose to advertise using the CPM model, you pay a specified amount for every 1,000 times your ad is displayed to users on the platform.

CPM is a commonly used metric in digital advertising to gauge the cost-effectiveness of an ad campaign. It helps advertisers understand how much they are paying to reach a thousand viewers of their ad. This model is particularly useful for campaigns focused on brand awareness and visibility, where the primary goal is to expose the ad to as many people as possible.

For instance, if you are running a Facebook ad campaign with a CPM of $5, it means you're paying $5 for every 1,000 times your ad is shown. It's important to note that CPM does not account for other metrics like clicks or conversions; it purely measures the cost of exposure.

But Rob, "why is there an 'M' in the name?" Glad you asked. The M stands for "Mille" which is Latin for 1000. "Rob, why do digital advertisers use a 2700-year-old abbreviation that no one knows unless they Google it?" Stop asking questions, nerd.

Clicks - I know what you are thinking…I know what a click is, why are you defining it? As you will see in the following paragraphs, you may think you know what a click is, but Facebook's definition of a click may be a bit different.

Facebook has 6 different measurements of "Clicks": Clicks (all), Link Clicks, Unique Lick Clicks, Outbound Clicks, Unique Outbound Clicks, and Unique Clicks (all). Who knew there were so many flavors of clicks? Baskin Robbins, eat your heart out. Let's see what they mean and why they list them out separately.

Clicks (all) - This metric count every possible click on any element of your ad, this includes CTA link clicks, clicks to your business page, post reactions (such as likes and loves), comments or shares, and clicks to "see more" of your ad copy. This is a total measure of all click engagement on your ad.

Unique Clicks (all) - This measures the number of unique people that performed any click on your ad.

Link Clicks - this counts the number of clicks on a link that leads to an advertiser-specified location. In this metric, clicks to your business page, post reactions, comments, and expanded ad copy are not counted. This metric is a better measure of clicks that lead users closer to the goal of your campaign.

Unique Link Clicks - This measures the amount of unique people that performed a link click.

Outbound Clicks - The number of clicks on links that lead to destinations outside Meta technologies like websites, app stores, or off-platform shops.

Unique Outbound Clicks - This measures the number of unique people who performed an outbound click.

CPC (Cost Per Click) - This metric represents the cost of each click on your ad. Essentially, it tells you how much you are paying on average for a user to click on your ad. CPC is calculated by dividing the total cost of the ad by the total number of clicks. For example, if you spend $100 on your ad and receive 50 clicks, your CPC would be $2.00. This metric is particularly important for campaigns where the goal is to drive traffic to a website or landing page, as it helps in evaluating the cost-efficiency of achieving that goal.

CTR (Click-Through Rate): CTR is a measure of how effective your ad is at getting people to take the action of clicking on it. It is calculated by dividing the total number of clicks your ad receives by the total number of impressions (times the ad is shown), and then multiplying the result by 100 to get a percentage. For instance, if your ad receives 100 clicks out of 10,000 impressions, your CTR would be 1%. A high CTR indicates that your ad is more relevant and engaging to the audience it's being shown to. CTR is a crucial measure of your ad's performance.

You can choose to view CPC & CTR for all 6 click types.

Key Metrics to Keep an Eye On

Now that you have a good understanding of what each of these metrics means, we can talk about how to use these metrics to evaluate your ad campaign's performance. We are going to focus on three main areas of metrics to give you a good overall look at performance. They are delivery, engagement, and performance.

Delivery metrics focus on how your ads are being shown to your audience. In the Meta ads platform, there is a specific column called "delivery" which shows the status of the campaign. That is not what I mean when I talk about delivery metrics. The ones I like to look at in this area are Impressions, reach, and CPM. I like to look at impressions, reach, and CPM together as they paint a good picture of how well your ads are being distributed. Impressions show you how many ads are being served a day, reach shows you how many unique people saw your ads, and CPM shows you the cost per 1000 impressions. It is important not to overanalyze these numbers by themselves because delivery on its own is not a good measure of overall performance unless your main goal is awareness or brand building. In that case, these numbers will give you great data on how you are accomplishing that goal.

Looking at impressions and reach numbers together shows you how many unique views your ad has. The closer the two numbers (reach and impressions) the more unique views or people who have seen your ad. If your numbers are vastly different, that means that your ads are being viewed by the same people multiple times, which is fine if that is what you want, but if you want the most unique views, the numbers should be close to the same.

CPM will show you how much Facebook is charging you to deliver your ad. If you have a $30 CPM that means that every time your ad is delivered 1000 times, you get charged $30. The lower the CPM, the more ads will get delivered to your audience. CPM for Facebook and Instagram ads can fluctuate for several different reasons. Understanding these things can help you make your ad campaigns better and more cost-effective. Here's a simple breakdown.

> Who You Target: If your ad targets a very specific group of people, it might cost more. The more details you add (like age, and interests), the more it can cost.

> How Good Your Ad Is: If people like, comment, or share your ad a lot, it might cost less because Facebook and Instagram think it's a good ad. But if people don't interact much with your ad, it can cost more.

> Your Ad Strategy: The way you want Facebook to optimize your campaign (like trying to get conversions or leads) can

affect how much you pay. When you target goals that focus on high-priority business outcomes, it can cost more to show your ads to these valuable targets.

Time of the Year: During busy times like holidays, the cost can go up because more businesses are advertising.

Where Your Ad Shows: Different places where your ad can show (like in the news feed or stories) are priced differently. Spots where more people might see and interact with your ad usually cost more.

Competition: If lots of advertisers are trying to reach the same people as you, it can make the cost go up.

Type of Ad: Different kinds of ads (like videos or pictures) can affect the cost. Really interesting and engaging ads usually get more engagement and might cost less.

Where People Are: Ads targeting people in busy areas, like big cities or high-income areas, might cost more.

Devices: If your ad is for specific devices like phones or desktops, it can change the cost. This depends on how people use these devices.

Your Industry: If you're in a market where lots of businesses are advertising similar things, it might cost more.

Engagement Metrics

Engagement metrics measure how your audience interacts with your ad. Some of the popular engagement metrics include likes, comments, shares, clicks, click-through rates, and video views. Like delivery metrics, the importance of a particular engagement metric is directly connected to the goal of your campaign. If your goal is engagement, then obviously these metrics will be weighed more heavily in terms of importance. Since most of our clients run campaigns that lead to some sort of business outcome, I will focus on the engagement metrics that contribute more to those actions. The ones I like to follow are link clicks, outbound link clicks, click-through rate, and cost per click.

Link clicks show you how many times people click on links that go to an advertiser-specified area, like a business page, website, or landing page. These show you the "valuable" clicks that resulted in someone learning more about your business or offer. If you are running a campaign that leads to an "off-platform" website or experience, outbound link clicks show you how many times people clicked on links that lead to your off-platform page. It is important to note that you could see a difference in outbound clicks and visits to your website or landing page, so be sure to verify that number with whatever platform you are using to track your web visits to know the more accurate count. For both of these metrics, it shows you the amount of people who showed intent on learning more about your product or service.

Knowing the total volume of clicks is good, but it doesn't tell you the whole story when it comes to evaluating performance. That is where click-through rate and cost per click come into play. Click-through rate or (CTR) is the percentage of times people saw your ad and then clicked on it. It helps you understand how effective your ad is at getting people's attention and encouraging them to take action. A higher CTR means that your ad is very good at converting attention to action, and a low CTR means that people may not be connecting with your message enough to take action. Average CTRs vary, so it is hard to say what is "good" or "bad". The average CTR for Meta ad campaigns is around 1%, so you can use that as a benchmark to see how your ads are performing.

Cost per Click (CPC) is a way of measuring how much you pay every time someone clicks on your ad. Technically, Facebook charges you for ads based on CPM, but CPC is a way of breaking down that cost by dividing the volume of clicks by the amount of money you spend on ad impressions. CPC is an important metric because it tells you how much you're spending to get people to take action on your ads, which in most cases is the purpose of running ads on Facebook and Instagram in the first place. When you first start running ads, this should be your main area of concern. The more people you send to your website or offer, the better chance you have of selling your product or service. That is why maximizing the clicks on your ad for the amount of money in your budget is the most important thing you should focus on when looking to optimize your campaign.

If you are wondering what is a "good" or "bad" CPC, that is a tricky question to answer because the value of traffic may be different for all businesses. If your business has a high ticket price, you can afford to spend more, and vice versa if you have a lower-cost offer. You know your business best so you should have an idea of what you feel comfortable paying for someone to learn more about your offer. Benchmarks vary based on industry and campaign objectives with ecommerce clicks averaging about 50 cents a click whereas finance and banking offers could be as high as $4 per click.

Conversion Metrics

Conversion metrics are used to track how well your ads are leading to specific actions or goals you've set, like making a purchase, signing up for a newsletter, or downloading an app. Here are the metrics we like to keep an eye on to see if campaigns are delivering on their chosen goals.

Results: The results metric in the Meta ads platforms is a measure of the performance goal you choose when setting up the campaign. If you selected Leads, then the results column will count leads, if you chose clicks, the results column will count clicks, and so on. With results, you will get a view of the total amount of the goal you want to receive from your campaign over a given period.

Cost Per Result: This tells you how much it costs, on average, to get one person to complete the desired action (like a sale or sign-up). If you spent $100 on your ad impressions and got 10 results (like 10 sales), your cost per result would be $10. This is the second major metric that we tell new advertisers to focus on when they start running a campaign, the other being cost per click. If you choose the correct conversion goal for your campaign, here is where you can see how well the ad campaign is delivering that goal against the budget you allocated. The allowable cost per result will vary from business to business. You should know what you are willing to spend to make a sale or get a lead, the cost-per-result metric should match that range.

These metrics are really important because they tell you not just if people are interested in your ad, but if they're taking the action you want them to take. By understanding your conversion metrics, you can see how effective your ads are at driving real results and can make better decisions about how to spend your ad budget.

Are you using a preset set of metrics, or did you create your view?
Let us know if you are still confused or need help seeing the right
metrics.

What are the key one or two metrics that you chose to focus on for
tracking and why?

Are there any metrics you are worried are not performing well, why
do you believe it is not working?

<u>**Key Takeaways:**</u>

There are hundreds of metrics to choose from when you are analyzing a campaign. Start small and try to focus on what is most important to your business's success.

Make sure you are considering the delivery, engagement, and performance metrics together to tell the whole story.

Each part of your ad campaign can show different metrics, make sure you look at each level (Campaign, ad set, and ad) when looking at campaign performance

Chapter 14:
Testing & Optimization

Optimizing your Facebook and Instagram ads is a lot like being a parent. It requires constant attention and care to ensure everything stays healthy and behaves as planned. But, if you take your eye off of it for too long, it will end up doing the complete opposite of what you wanted in the first place. In the world of social media advertising, this means continuously working on and improving your ads to get the best possible results. Like parenting, it is hard to know exactly what to do as every situation is different, especially if you're just starting. Here is the advice I wish I had when I first started running ad campaigns, so at least you will have a head start.

Always Be Ready to Make Changes: Think of your ads like a recipe you're trying to perfect. You might need to adjust the ingredients from time to time. This could mean changing the pictures or videos in your ads, trying out different headlines, or tweaking the words in your ad to make them more appealing. Each small change can make a big difference.

Understand How People React to Your Ads: It's important to see how people are responding. Are they clicking on your ad? Do they like or share it? Are they taking the action you want, like buying your product or signing up for more information? By understanding this, you can get a sense of what's working and what's not.

Learn From the Data: Facebook and Instagram provide lots of useful information about how your ads are performing. We reviewed a lot of great metrics in Chapter 11. While this might seem overwhelming at first, it's really valuable. You have metrics that tell you how many people are seeing your ads, how many are taking action, and even who these people are. Use this data to guide your optimizations.

Keep Up with Changes: Social media platforms are always evolving. They introduce new features, change their algorithms, and update their policies. It's important to stay informed about these changes because they can affect how your ads perform.

Watch Your Budget: Be mindful of how much you're spending. It's not just about spending more; it's about spending wisely. Put more of your budget into the ads that are working well, and less into those that aren't.

Seek Feedback and Improve: Sometimes, it helps to get a fresh perspective. Don't hesitate to ask for feedback on your ads from friends, colleagues, or even your social media followers. Use this feedback to make your ads even better.

Testing

One of the most important parts of optimizing your ad campaigns is testing. Testing is the art of experimenting with various elements of your ad campaigns to determine what works best in engaging your audience and achieving your marketing objectives. In the fast-paced world of digital advertising, especially on platforms like Facebook and Instagram, things are constantly changing. The kinds of ads that people respond to, the latest trends, and how these platforms show your ads can all change pretty quickly. By testing your ads regularly, you can adapt to these changes and make sure your ads are always performing well.

Why Testing Matters in Facebook & Instagram Advertising

Testing your ads on Facebook and Instagram is important for a few reasons. First, every group of people you're advertising to is different. What catches one group's attention might not work for another. By testing, you can figure out exactly what each group likes and doesn't like, and then make ads that fit them perfectly.

Another big plus of testing is that it helps you better spend your ad budget. When you find out which ads get the best results, you can put more of your budget into those and not waste money on ads that don't work as well. This way, you get more bang for your buck.

Also, things on social media change all the time – new trends pop up, and what people like can shift quickly. By testing your ads regularly, you can keep up with these changes and make sure your ads are always hitting the mark. Plus, every time you test an ad, you learn something new. You get to see not only what works, but you also start to understand why some things work better than others. This helps make your ads better over time.

Types of Tests for Your Facebook and Instagram Ads:

Testing does not have to be complicated. If you have an ad running and you are unhappy with its performance, you can simply change a component of that ad and evaluate the change by seeing the difference in ad metrics before and after the change. This is commonly called a "Pre / Post" test or method.

Another testing method is called split testing. This is a simple but powerful way to test your ads. You create two versions of the same ad, but change just one thing - like the picture, the headline, or the call-to-action. By comparing how the two versions perform, you can see which one element works better.

What Elements Should You Test in Your Ads?

There are a lot of things you can test to try to get better performance from your ads, including your ad creative, copy, CTA, buttons, audience, and placements. Although all of them are important, some have a bigger effect on performance than others. For our clients, this is the order of importance for testing ads. Feel free to try any of these in your campaigns, but we have seen that going in this order helps get the biggest results, fastest.

Ad Images and Videos: People respond strongly to visuals. Try using different images or videos to see which ones grab your audience's attention.

Ad Copy: The words in your ad are crucial. Experiment with different headlines, body text, and
CTA phrases. Small tweaks in wording can sometimes lead to big improvements in performance.

CTA Buttons: The CTA is what prompts people to take action, like making a purchase or signing up. Test different CTAs to find out which one encourages more people to click.

Target Audiences: Play around with targeting different demographics, interests, and behaviors. Sometimes, targeting a slightly different audience can yield better results.

Ad Placement: Facebook and Instagram offer various places to show your ads, like in the news feed, stories, or in-stream videos. Testing different placements helps you find out where your ads are most effective.

Setting Up Your Ad Tests Properly

When setting up your tests, consider these points:
One Change at a Time: When testing ads, it's important to only change one element per version so you can see which change made the difference.

Define Clear Goals: Before you start testing, know what you're trying to improve. Is it more clicks, more conversions, or something else?
Ensure Your Test Is Valid: You need enough people to see your test to make sure your results are reliable. This means considering factors like the size of your audience and the duration of your test.

Budget Wisely: Make sure you allocate enough budget so that both versions of your ad get a fair chance to be seen by your audience.

Analyzing Your Test Results

After your tests have run for a while, it's time to analyze the results. Look at key metrics like click-through rate, conversion rate, and engagement. Ask yourself: Which version of the ad performed better? What do these results tell you about your audience's preferences and behaviors? Use these insights to make informed decisions about your future ad strategies.

Optimizing your Facebook and Instagram ads is a continuous journey of testing, learning, and improving. It's about being attentive to both the big picture and the small details, and always being ready to adapt and refine your approach. With patience and persistence, you'll see your efforts pay off in better-performing ads.

Questions: Post Your Answers in our Free group at facebook.com/groups/fbinsta101

What tests are you planning to run for your campaign? If you need help thinking of one, post and let us know.

Were there any interesting data insights that led you to choose these tests? If you have trouble thinking about how to do this, let us know.

<u>**Key Takeaways:**</u>

Tests should always be driven by data insight and set up to improve that metric. For example, if your ad has a low CTR, you could test the Headline, ad copy, or image to see if you can increase your CTR percentage.

Do not test more than one element at a time. If you do this, you will not know for certain what led to the change in performance.

Do not be discouraged if a test performs worse than the original version. It is as important to know what doesn't work as it is to know what does.

Chapter 15:
Future Trends and Predictions in Facebook Ads

Welcome to the crystal ball chapter, where we peek into the future of Facebook ads. With the digital landscape evolving faster than a viral TikTok dance, staying ahead of the curve is key. So, queue the smoke machine, dim the lights, and let's explore what the future might hold for Facebook advertising.

Understanding Facebook's Algorithm for Advertising

Facebook's algorithm has changed a lot since it started, and these changes are really important for anyone advertising on the platform. In simple terms, the algorithm is like a set of rules that decides which posts people see on their Facebook feed. At first, Facebook's algorithm was pretty simple. It mostly showed people's posts from their friends and family. For advertisers, this meant trying to create ads that got likes, comments, and shares. The more people interacted with your ad, the more it would be shown. As Facebook got bigger, the algorithm started to get more complex. It began to look at what type of posts people liked – were they photos, videos, or text? It also started considering how new a post was and how close the person posting was to the viewer. For advertisers, this meant thinking more about what kind of content to create and how often to post it.

Machine Learning and Predicting Interests

A big change came when Facebook started using machine learning. This means the algorithm could get smart about guessing what each person might like to see. It looked at how people behaved on Facebook – what they liked, clicked on, and spent time reading. For advertisers, this meant that Facebook could get good at showing your ads to people who are most likely to be interested in them. Lately, Facebook has been trying to make sure that the stuff in people's feeds is meaningful. The algorithm now favors posts that create conversations and meaningful interactions, like comments and shares. For advertisers, this means creating ads that engage people and encourage them to interact. Facebook has also been dealing with fake news and ensuring ads are truthful and ethical. This means the algorithm now tries to avoid showing misleading or harmful content.

The Future of AI and Machine Learning in Facebook and Instagram Ads

In the future, AI (Artificial Intelligence) and Machine Learning are going to become a much bigger part of ads on Facebook and Instagram. AI is going to get even better at figuring out what each person likes. So, in the future, the ads you see might feel like they were made just for you, based on what you usually like and do on these platforms. AI will not only look at what you liked in the past but also try to guess what you might like or do next. This means advertisers can show you ads that match what you might be looking for, even before you know to start looking.

AI might start helping to make the actual content of the ads, like writing the text for you or creating pictures and videos on the fly. This could make ads more interesting and fun to interact with. AI in ads might start working with cool new tech like Augmented Reality (AR) and Virtual Reality (VR). This could mean you can interact with ads in a way that feels more real, like trying on glasses or seeing how a new sofa might look in your living room, but through your screen.

So, AI and Machine Learning are going to change the way ads work on Facebook and Instagram. They'll make ads more personal, more interesting, and more effective. For people making ads, it will be important to keep up with these changes to make the best ads they can.

The Growing Importance of Video Content in Facebook
Advertising

In recent years, video content has rapidly become a cornerstone
of digital advertising, and its influence is set to expand further,
particularly on platforms like Facebook. Video ads are becoming
more prevalent and impactful, mirroring the influence once held by
traditional television commercials. These ads offer a dynamic way
to capture attention in a user's news feed, where static images
and text once reigned. The shift is driven by users' preferences for
engaging, easily digestible content that videos provide.

But why are video ads becoming so popular? For one, the visual
and auditory nature of video makes it an incredibly effective
medium for storytelling. Brands can convey emotions, showcase
products in action, and create narratives that resonate with
viewers on a deeper level. Additionally, advancements in
technology have made creating high-quality videos more
accessible and cost-effective than ever before.

The format of video ads is also evolving. From short, snappy clips
designed for quick consumption to longer, more immersive
experiences, the variety of video ads on Facebook caters to a
broad spectrum of marketing goals. This includes everything from
brief product highlights to extensive brand storytelling.

One of the most exciting developments in video content is the rise
of live streaming and interactive ads. Live streaming on Facebook
isn't just for influencers and content creators; it's becoming a
powerful tool for brands too. Imagine watching a live stream of a
product launch, where you can ask questions in real-time, or
participating in a live demo of a cooking gadget.

Interactive ads take this a step further. They're not just about watching; they're about participating. These ads can include features like clickable elements, where viewers can, for example, change the color of a product they're viewing, or make choices that influence the ad's storyline. It's a level of engagement that goes beyond passive viewing, creating a more immersive and memorable experience.

Building on this interactivity, we're seeing the emergence of real-time shopping experiences within video ads – a digital nod to the likes of QVC. Viewers can watch a product demonstration and make purchases directly through the video, all in real-time. This seamless integration of content and commerce not only simplifies the shopping experience but also adds a layer of excitement and immediacy to online shopping.

As video content continues to grow in importance, advertisers must adapt. This means not only creating compelling video content but also understanding how to leverage the unique features of live and interactive formats. Staying ahead in this dynamic space requires creativity, a willingness to experiment, and a keen eye on emerging trends and technologies.

Lynnesight: Hearing the importance of video content may make you think you need a huge production studio setup, expensive editing tools, or even the need to hire additional people to create these videos. While it is important to have good lighting (which could just mean natural light) and clear quality, the majority of people prefer real, authentic videos to overproduced videos. If they think they are hearing from real people with authentic experiences vs actors they are way more likely to respond positively and even purchase.

Staying Ahead by Embracing Adaptability

Adaptability in Facebook advertising is not just about reacting to changes; it's about anticipating them. This requires a mindset that is flexible, open to new ideas, and prepared for shifts in strategies. Remember, what works today may not work tomorrow. Platforms evolve, user preferences change and new features are introduced. Staying adaptable means continuously evaluating and adjusting your campaigns to align with these changes. Staying ahead in the game of Facebook advertising is about being adaptable, continuously learning, and staying attuned to the latest developments. It's a journey that requires commitment, curiosity, and a creative spirit. By embracing these qualities, you will be well-equipped to navigate the ever-changing world of digital advertising, ensuring your campaigns are not only successful but also innovative and engaging.

Questions: Post Your Answers in our Free group at facebook.com/groups/fbinsta101

What future trend interests you the most and why?

Do you think there will be other future trends in advertising? What are they?

If you could wave your magic wand and make any kind of advertising on Facebook or Instagram happen, what would that look like?

<u>**Key Takeaways:**</u>

The algorithm that controls what you see on Facebook changes constantly. Be sure to keep an eye out for trends you are seeing in content and ads.

AI and machine learning are becoming a bigger part of Facebook and Instagram advertising every day. Be sure to keep testing and learning as they add new features to stay up to date.

Video has been becoming more and more popular on social media, you should be prepared for this future and begin experimenting with video in your content and ads.

Embrace adaptability. The key to success in Facebook and Instagram ads is to roll with the changes and never get too comfortable doing things the same way.

Chapter 16 -
The End of the Zucking Book

Great job on finishing the book! We hope it helps you grow your business with your Facebook and Instagram ads. When I first thought about writing this, I knew that people running small businesses could benefit from social media ads. But many people told me they thought it was too hard, too technical, too expensive, or that they needed to hire a professional agency. I wrote this book to show you that's not true. You don't need to be an expert or have a lot of money to make good ads. I wanted to explain everything in a simple, easy-to-understand way, so you wouldn't get bored or lost. My goal was to help you feel confident about using social media ads to grow your business, and I hope that's what you've gained from reading this.

In this book, you've picked up a bunch of important stuff about Facebook and Instagram ads, especially how great they are for small businesses. You've learned how to set up a Facebook Business Page, the different ways you can run ads, and how to put together your ad account. We went through how to create a strategy for your ads, how to get an ad campaign up and running, and then how to keep an eye on how well it's doing. You now know about understanding all those numbers and stats (metrics and analytics), and how to make your ads better by testing and tweaking them. Plus, we even took a quick look at what might be coming next in the world of online ads.

Looking back, it's pretty cool to see how much you've learned from this book. But this is just the beginning. There's so much more to discover about advertising on Facebook and Instagram. The hardest part was just getting started, but now you're on your way and know a thing or two about how it all works.

I hope you see how useful all this stuff you've learned can be once you put it into action. There are businesses out there that went from making just a few sales every week to earning millions of dollars. And guess what? They did it all by using Facebook and Instagram ads. The coolest part? These companies started just like you are now. The only thing they did differently was they got started a bit sooner.

So, don't wait around to use what you've learned. You might be only one good ad campaign away from having the best year your business has ever seen. Think about it, with the right Facebook or Instagram ad, you could reach a ton of new customers and boost your sales. It's pretty exciting! So go ahead and give it a try, and you could see some amazing results for your business.

I'd like to send out a special thanks to Lynne, my co-author, business partner, and wife. I can with 100% confidence say that I would have never even thought of writing a book, let alone finish one, without her help and encouragement along the way. Hopefully, you will get to meet us when you join our free Facebook group or if you would like to work with us in the future.

I'd also like to thank Tina Torres, our publishing coach. Tina is an amazing person and is absolutely the best at what she does. If you have ever considered writing a book about anything. Be sure to reach out to her to get started.

Remember that old saying, "The journey of a thousand miles begins with a single step"? Well, it's true, especially when it comes to Facebook and Instagram ads. Starting something new can feel big and a bit scary. You might be worried that you still don't know enough, but don't let these harmful and inaccurate thoughts stop you!

We believe in you. You've got this! Just take that first small step. Start by creating your first ad campaign. It doesn't have to be perfect. What's important is that you're trying and learning. Each ad you create is a step forward, and every time you do it, you'll learn something new. This is how you'll get better and better.

So, don't be held back by the thought that it's too complex, too confusing, or too scary. Lots of people have been where you are now, and they've gone on to do great things with their ads. And you can too. Just take that first step and start your journey. Before you know it, you'll be reaching customers and growing your business in ways you never thought possible.

Best of all, we are here to help! I hope by now you joined our free Facebook group, introduced yourself, and posted answers to the questions and topics covered in the book. If you haven't, what are you waiting for? It's free.

We also offer advanced group coaching, one-on-one consulting, and agency services if you or someone you know is looking for help with Facebook ads from a down-to-earth couple whose mission is to help small businesses grow and reach their full potential.

Happy advertising and we hope to meet and talk to you soon!

-Rob & Lynne Alfano